THOMAS EDISON:

The Great American Inventor

SOLUTIONS
◆

THOMAS EDISON:
The Great American Inventor

BY LOUISE EGAN

Illustrated by Frank Riccio

Barron's Educational Series, Inc.

First edition published 1987
by Barron's Educational Series, Inc.

All inquiries should be addressed to:
Barron's Educational Series, Inc.
250 Wireless Blvd.
Hauppauge, NY 11788

Library of Congress Catalog Card No. 87-19558

International Standard Book No. 0-8120-3922-X

Library of Congress Cataloging-in-Publication Data

Egan, Louise.
    Thomas Alva Edison: great American inventor.
    (Solutions)
    Bibliography.
    Includes index.
    Summary: Examines the life and achievements of the famous inventor,
from his boyhood experiments to his search for electricity.
    1. Edison, Thomas A. (Thomas Alva), 1847–1931—
Juvenile literature.   2. Inventors—United States—
Biography—Juvenile literature.   [1. Edison, Thomas A.
(Thomas Alva), 1847–1931.   2. Inventors]   I. Title.
II. Series: Solutions (New York, N.Y.)
TK140.E3E35   1987   621.3′092′4 [B] [92]   87-19558
ISBN 0-8120-3922-X

Printed in the United States of America

56   969   98

CONTENTS

Curious and Carefree

M ama! Mama! Look—what are those?"
"Those are covered wagons, dear. They're heading to California."

"Where's that?"

"Out West—way, way west of here, where the gold is."

"What's gold?"

Mrs. Edison smiled at her three-year-old son as she answered his question. He must have asked a hundred questions today! she thought. But that was good. She wanted Tom to learn.

Thomas Alva Edison, also called Alva or Al, was the youngest and most inquisitive of the Edison children. He seemed to have been born asking questions.

"What makes birds fly?" "Why does water put out fire?" "What makes the sky blue?" Young Tom took nothing for granted. Though Tom often wore his father out with questions, Mrs. Edison was more patient.

Mrs. Edison watched her son as he gazed out the

The wagon train rolls by Milan, Ohio.

window. Three large covered wagons were lumbering slowly down the dusty main road of Milan, Ohio. The year was 1850, and America was just beginning to grow.

At that time, pioneers had just begun to settle in California, the thirty-first state. Settlers were still fighting with the Indians over control of the Plains. And the railroad lines were gradually moving out from the East with the first steam-driven locomotives.

Because train lines were only beginning to be built, ships and barges were used to transport food and materials across the country. If a town was near a large lake or river, a canal was built for the ships to come through. In 1850, Tom Edison's hometown, Milan, was one of the busiest canal towns in the country.

The Edisons' house was at the top of a hill overlooking the canal. Tom's favorite playground was the terrace outside the kitchen, where he could keep an eye on all that went on below. There were the ships and barges on the canal, whose captains could often be heard singing hearty songs about river life. There was also a large flour mill, a brewery, grain storage elevators, a tannery and a blacksmith shop. Farmers with wagons full of grain would drive their six-horse teams into Milan, cracking their whips and yelling, "Gee-haw!"

There was also Mr. Edison's lumberyard and shingle mill, where the roofs were made for the fourteen grain warehouses in the area. Four-year-old Tom liked to run down the slope to the lumberyard. There he would play with the discarded wood chips and shingles. He could entertain himself this way for hours, making roads and toy buildings. Sometimes, he would draw, sketching the shops and craft signs he saw around him.

Young Tom had fair hair, a round face and large blue

Covered wagons heading for California.

eyes that observed everything. One day he asked his mother, "Why does the neighbor's goose squat on her eggs?"

"To keep them warm," Mrs. Edison replied.

"Why does she keep them warm?"

"To hatch them, my dear."

"What does *hatch* mean?"

"It means letting the little geese come out of their shells, so they can be born."

"You mean, keeping the eggs warm makes the little geese come out?"

"Yes."

Mrs. Edison noticed the thoughtful look on her son's little face as he walked away. She smiled and returned to her chores.

Meanwhile, Tom wandered over to the neighbor's barn. The chicken and geese clucked and squawked as he walked in, but Tom was not going to harm them. In fact, he was only going to help. He dug a neat little nest in

4

Tom attempts to hatch goose eggs.

the hay and filled it with chicken and goose eggs; then he sat down. Five minutes passed, then ten, then twenty. The barn was nice and dark, and the sweet-smelling hay was warm. Before long, he was curled up fast asleep.

"Tom! There you are!"

Tom opened his eyes and saw his father standing over him in the barn. "What are you doing here?" Mr. Edison demanded. "We've been looking for you everywhere!"

Tom did not know what he had done wrong. "I was trying to hatch the eggs," he replied innocently. Tom thought that if a goose could hatch eggs, so could a person. He did not realize that nature does not work that way.

Mr. Edison wondered about his son. He was not like other boys. He had such strange ideas!

Tom was the youngest in the family by many years. When Tom was born, his brother, William Pitt, was fifteen and his sister, Harriet Ann, was fourteen. His eldest sister, Marion, married at the age of twenty-one, when Tom was just three. There had been three other children, but they had died as babies before Tom was born. Because he had no close brothers or sisters, and only a few friends near his age, Tom spent most of his time exploring and experimenting by himself.

These experiments would often get Tom in trouble. Sometimes Tom was plainly mischievous, but most of the time he did not mean to misbehave. It was just that he could never predict what would happen during his experiments. By the time Tom was six years old, he was known as a "problem" child, for he was forever getting into scrapes.

The worst of Tom's experiments took place one breezy afternoon in the Edison barn. Tom gathered some dry sticks together and soon had started a little fire inside the barn. Suddenly, the flames leaped out beyond the circle Tom had made. The breeze quickly carried the flames over the dirt and straw to the wooden walls—the barn was on fire! Tom dashed out safely, but the barn could not be saved. He watched as it burned to the ground.

Mr. Edison was furious. "What were you doing? How could you *do* such a thing?" he shouted angrily. "Do you realize the whole town could have burned down if there had been a strong wind?"

Tom did not know what to say. He did not dare tell his father he had just wanted to see what fire would do. His father never would have understood.

Mr. Edison was determined to punish Tom in a way that his son would never forget. In those days, boys were often whipped at home or in school when they had done something wrong. But it was unheard of for a boy to be whipped in public.

For that reason, a curious crowd gathered in Milan's cobblestoned square one morning. It was two days after the barn-burning, and a rare sight was taking place: little Tom Edison was receiving a public lashing from his father. Tom sobbed with each blow, until Mr. Edison considered the punishment equal to the crime.

It was a morning Tom never forgot, though years later he could look back on it and laugh. But if his father had wanted the public whipping to discourage Tom from doing any more experiments, the punishment had not worked at all. Tom Edison did not learn lessons easily from anyone but himself.

CHAPTER TWO

Educating Young Tom

When the railroad came to Ohio, life quickly changed for canal towns like Milan. Ships and barges were no longer needed to transport goods—trains could do it faster. Farmers started bringing their grain to towns where the train stopped. Soon no one came to Milan, and business was bad. Many townspeople were forced to leave town and seek their fortunes elsewhere. The Edisons were among those people.

In the spring of 1854, when Tom was seven years old, the Edisons traveled by train and horse-drawn carriage to Detroit, Michigan. From there, a paddleboat called *The Ruby* took them for a smooth ride up the St. Clair River to the small town of Port Huron, the Edisons' new home.

The paddleboat ride was lots of fun for a young boy from Ohio. The green forests along the river shore were bursting with life. There were sailboats and lake steamers of every kind. There were even canoes, guided by Indians dressed in feathers and beads. Tom enjoyed watching these Indians cut swiftly in and out of the paddleboat's course. He and his brothers and sisters could even sometimes see the smoke rising from Indian campfires in the woods.

The Edisons' new house was large, with carved balconies in front and big windows that looked out onto the lake and river. There was an apple orchard and a vegetable garden too. Tom found plenty to do there.

Mr. Edison built a wooden observation tower one hundred feet high that looked out onto the lakes and shoreline. Sometimes visitors came and paid twenty-five cents to climb up the tower and look through the telescope at the view. The most frequent visitor to the tower, however, was young Tom. Up high, where it was peaceful and quiet, Tom could watch all that happened down below. This was similar to what he had done as a toddler in Milan, where he watched the riverboats from the kitchen terrace. Tom learned about his world by looking and watching and asking questions about what he had seen.

Mr. Edison thought his son was somewhat peculiar, always playing by himself or asking endless amounts of ridiculous questions. But Mrs. Edison, who was once a schoolteacher, and understood children better than her husband did, believed Tom was a special and very bright boy.

Not long after the Edisons came to Port Huron, Tom became seriously ill with scarlet fever. Illness was not new to the family. At one time or another all of the Edisons had been sick with diseases like this. Tom's parents wanted their son to be well and strong before he started

The Ruby steams up the St. Clair River to Port Huron.

school. This is probably why they kept him home until the following September. By that time, Tom was eight and a half years old.

For a boy who was used to learning things his own way and to playing outside by himself all day long, sitting still in a one-room schoolhouse was pure misery. Tom did not like school one bit. His teacher, the Reverend G. B. Engle, and his wife made the children learn by memorizing their lessons and repeating them out loud. When a child forgot an answer, or had not studied well enough, Reverend Engle whipped the unfortunate pupil with a leather strap! Mrs. Engle also heartily approved of using the whip as a way of teaching students better study habits. Her whippings were often worse than her husband's!

Tom was confused by Reverend Engle's way of teaching. He could not learn through fear. Nor could he just sit and memorize. He liked to see things for himself and ask questions. But Reverend Engle grew as exasperated by Tom's questions as Mr. Edison did. For that reason, Tom learned very little in his first few months, and his grades were bad.

Years later, Tom would say of his school experience, "I remember I used to never be able to get along at school. I was always at the foot [bottom] of the class. I used to feel that the teachers did not sympathize with me, and that my father thought I was stupid."

One day, around Christmas, Tom overheard Reverend Engle say that the Edison boy's mind was "addled," or muddled and confused. This made Tom so angry that

Tom in school with the Rev. and Mrs. Engle.

he immediately stormed out of the schoolroom and ran home.

"I'm never going to go to school again!" Tom exclaimed to his surprised mother. Then he told her what the schoolmaster had said about him.

"Hmmph! 'Addled!' " said Mrs. Edison, suddenly as angry as Tom. Why, *addled* was the last thing in the world anyone could call her little boy!

The next morning Mrs. Edison went to school with Tom. She was determined to make Reverend Engle apologize for what he had said and admit that he had been wrong. Tom watched as an angry discussion broke out between his mother and the schoolmaster. It pleased Tom to see how his mother stood up for him.

"My son is *not* backward!" declared Mrs. Edison, adding, "and I believe I ought to know. I taught children once myself!" Despite her efforts, neither the Reverend nor Mrs. Engle would change their opinion of young Tom Edison. But Mrs. Edison was equally strong in her opinion. Finally, she realized what she had to do.

"All right," Mrs. Edison said, "I am hereby taking my son out of your school." Tom could hardly believe his ears! "I'll instruct him at home myself," he heard her say.

Tom looked up at his mother, this wonderful woman who believed in him. He promised himself that he would make his mother proud of him.

Tom's new "school" life at home was entirely different from his experiences in the wretched one-room schoolhouse.

Every morning, after Mrs. Edison had finished her first round of housecleaning, she would call Tom to his lessons. Without forcing him to learn, and by giving him lots of love and encouragement, she taught Tom reading, writing and arithmetic. The one subject that Tom never quite mastered was spelling. Why? It involved rules and memorization.

But anything that caught Tom's heart and imagination was something he could master, and Mrs. Edison seemed to know just how to inspire her son. Right from the start, she began to read to Tom—not the books popular among children Tom's age, but books that were difficult even for adults. Her list included *The Decline and Fall of the Roman Empire, The History of England* and *The History of the World.* She also read Tom classical literature, like the plays of William Shakespeare and the novels of Charles Dickens. By the time Tom was nine years old, he had begun to read these books by himself.

One day Mrs. Edison gave Tom a book that was different from anything either of them had ever read. Yet, for some reason, Mrs. Edison thought the book might interest her son. It was an elementary book on physical science, called R. G. Parker's *School of Natural Philosophy,* and it changed Tom's life.

This book contained all the scientific facts then known, covering everything from steam engines to gas-filled balloons. It also gave hundreds of different experiments that could be done at home. With that book, learning not only became a joy to Tom, it became a game.

Experiments were fun, ten-year-old Tom discov-

Tom continues his studies at home.

ered. He read R. G. Parker's book from beginning to end and tried out every experiment in it. Mrs. Edison then gave Tom an old copy of the *Dictionary of Science*, whose experiments he also eagerly performed. Before long, Tom's bedroom shelves were lined with different-sized bottles and jars of chemicals. Any pocket money Tom had, he used for buying more chemicals at the pharmacy or scraps of metal and wire at the junkyard.

Suddenly, Tom's whole life revolved around his chemistry experiments. Mr. Edison worried that Tom was spending too much time on only one thing. "Here's a penny, if you read a book of serious literature," Mr. Edison would say to Tom, flashing a copper coin in his hand. Tom would always take the penny and then read a difficult, serious book—but the pennies were always put toward buying more chemicals.

Mrs. Edison was less concerned about Tom's dedication to chemistry. She was happy to see him following what seemed to be his natural path. What did bother her was the mess the chemicals made of her house, and it frequently caused her to lose her temper. "Thomas Alva! Just look at this! I don't know what this is—"

"Sulfuric acid, from the wet-cell battery, Mother."

"Just look at how this sulfuric acid you spilled has ruined the chair!"

Eventually, Tom was forced to move his bedroom laboratory to the cellar. Alone down in his lab, Tom could spend hours studying simple chemicals and gases or learning other areas of science.

Though Tom's favorite things to do were different from the pastimes of other boys his age, he was just as high-spirited and mischievous as any of his friends. This boyishness sometimes affected his experiments. Once, for example, he read about Benjamin Franklin's discoveries with static electricity. (Static electricity is, for example, the spark you get during winter when you touch a doorknob after walking on a wool rug.) Tom's experiment involved rubbing the fur of two big tomcats, whose tails he had attached to wires. The result of that experiment, however, only left Tom with severe claw marks.

Still, electricity intrigued Tom. At that time, very

little was known about it, and electricity was not a part of people's everyday lives. There were oil lamps for indoor lights, but those gave off a bad smell and were more expensive to use than candles. Wood-burning stoves and fireplaces were still the only sources of heat for homes and buildings. Reading books was the way people entertained themselves before television and movie theaters. Before there were telephones, people wrote letters and had other people deliver messages for them on foot. And before there were radios, people just made their own music.

Yet there did exist one fairly recent invention that used electricity for a practical, everyday purpose. This invention was the telegraph. It was shaped like a box, with a handle to tap out messages. This little machine was actually a whole communications system. Like today's telephones, each telegraph machine was connected to other machines by wires; messages were sent and received by electrical impulses. Telegraph operators would tap out messages on the machine in Morse code. This code was invented by the telegraph's creator, Samuel Morse. To replace letters and numbers, which could not be sent on the machine, Morse invented a code using short and long tapping patterns. These patterns came through as sounds.

Each letter had its own pattern. Written down, A, B, and C in Morse code appeared like this:

A · —
B – ···
C – · — ·

Samuel Morse's 1844 telegraph key.

Patterns of dots and dashes made up the rest of the alphabet too. The name, Edison, for example, looked like this:

.   — ..   ..   ———   — .
E   D   I   S   O   N

The sound of a dot could be distinguished from the sound of a dash, because the sound of a dot was much shorter than that of a dash.

In Tom's day, the telegraph machine was as new and fascinating to young boys as computers and video machines are today. Every boy dreamed of being a telegraph operator, an occupation that to them meant "adventure!" Telegraph operators roamed across the country, extending the telegraph wires over the mountains and prairies, through Indian country, to the California coast.

For that reason, many boys were inspired to set up simple, homemade telegraphs of their own. Tom Edison was among those boys. After reading about an example in a popular science handbook, he got hold of some wire normally used for holding up stovepipes and stretched it from his house, through the woods, to a friend's house. To keep the sound moving, he used small bottles pegged on thin nails that were driven into trees. Tom thought this worked fine, though his friend did not always receive a clear message. When the message could not be understood, the friend would call out from his house, "What did you say?" This frustrated Tom no end.

Tom's early boyhood days were intensely happy ones. He was an all-American boy who just happened to prefer tinkering with batteries, telegraphs, chemicals, and even toy steam engines to playing outdoor games. He was full of energy and able to learn from his mistakes. Down in the cellar, accidents often occurred, with little explosions going off from time to time.

"He's going to blow us up!" Tom could hear his father shout from upstairs.

"Now, hush!" Mrs. Edison would reply. "Tom knows what he's doing."

But as Tom's experiments got more and more complex, he realized he needed more than mere pocket money to support them. Mrs. Edison helped Tom and his friend, Michael Oates, lay out and grow a large vegetable garden. They then hired a horse and cart to bring their onions, lettuce, cabbages and peas to market. But neither Tom nor Michael thought much of working under the hot sun for such long hours. By the end of the summer, the two had made about three hundred dollars; but for Tom, the money was not enough to make up for all the work he had done. He wanted to do something else, but he was not sure what.

Then the railroad came to Port Huron and everything changed.

CHAPTER THREE

Tom the Newsboy

T he railroad, with its enormous, brightly painted train cars, caused quite a stir among the townfolk when it steamed from Detroit into Port Huron in 1859. Trains were the newest, most modern link to other parts of the country. The people in Port Huron were excited to think that their little town was part of the growing, national railroad network. On top of that, many of them had never even seen a train until that first, huge, iron and brass locomotive swept majestically into the Port Huron station.

But even before the train's arrival, Tom had learned that the daily train between Detroit and Port Huron was looking for someone to be a newsboy. A newsboy would sell newspapers, as well as food and sweets to the passengers. Tom was only twelve then, and Mrs. Edison was strongly against his going to work. But Mr. Edison's own business ventures had not done well in Port Huron, and the family had very little money. They could not afford to send Tom to school, and Tom did not want to go anyway. He had spent four years under his mother's guidance and had learned how to teach himself. He felt ready for a job.

Still Mrs. Edison shook her head.

"But, Mother," said Tom, "there's a long layover in Detroit every day. I could use that time to read books, and with the money I earn, I'll be able to keep up my science studies."

"The boy's got a point," Mr. Edison said, looking at his wife.

Mrs. Edison looked back at her husband and then at Tom. Finally, she hung her head and stared down at her lap, blinking back her tears.

Mr. Edison tapped Tom on the knee, and the two went out of the room. Later, Mr. Edison went down to the station and spoke with the railroad people about a job for his son. By the time the first train rolled into Port Huron, Tom Edison was anxiously waiting to start as newsboy on the daily train.

The Grand Trunk Railway, which carried both passengers and freight, left Port Huron each morning at seven o'clock. By then, the young, fair-haired newsboy with the solid, square jaw and big smile would be on board carrying a large basket brimming with goods.

"Newspapers, apples, sandwiches, molasses, peanuts!" Tom would call as he made his way from car to car. His customers included all kinds of people—farmers, workers, newly arrived immigrants and sometimes beautifully dressed tourists.

The crowds of passengers were always changing, with people constantly getting on and off the train. Tom enjoyed having each day be different from the one before. He also found it thrilling to work in a place that moved at an incredible thirty miles an hour!

Tom as a newsboy for the Grand Trunk Railway.

The train on which Tom sold newspapers and refreshments.

The Grand Trunk Railway took more than three hours to reach Detroit, which was sixty-three miles south of Port Huron. The train remained in the Detroit station until early evening, when it made the trip back to Port Huron. These were long hours for a twelve-year-old, especially one who had been up before dawn and often did not get home until ten or eleven at night. His first week's earnings came to one dollar a day.

Even Tom felt he should be earning more than that, and before long he came up with a way to add to his wage. He was a friendly and honest boy. Store merchants were happy to help him out, especially when it benefitted them as well. So Tom was able to make a deal with the town grocer and, with the conductor's permission, carried fresh butter, berries, vegetables and fruit in the baggage car of the train. He sold these items along with his regular goods at the different stops along the route. This was so successful that soon Tom had other boys working for him, and he was earning almost twenty dollars a week!

During the long layover in Detroit each day Tom watched and learned much about railroad life. He watched the men as they switched train cars, repaired valves and fixed steam boilers. He also observed the telegraph operators, who were just beginning to signal the various train movements between stations.

Wandering around Detroit, Tom was able to watch the activities of a small but booming city. He spoke with men in machine shops, and he even had a little money to buy books or science equipment.

The worst part of the day came once he got back to Port Huron. Tom did not like driving his horse and cart home in the dark. He was especially terrified of driving past a stretch of deep, dark woods that was the site of the soldiers' graveyard. Whenever he reached that spot, he would close his eyes and whip the horse. They would streak swiftly past the graveyard, Tom's heart pounding furiously all the while. Eventually, however, Tom realized that nothing ever happened there, and his fear of the dark and the graveyard disappeared.

All in all, Tom would later recall this period as the happiest time of his life. "I was just old enough to have a good time in the world," he said, "but not old enough to understand any of its troubles."

One morning Tom was on the train platform selling newspapers before the train pulled out of the station. While a customer was fishing in his pockets for the proper change, Tom suddenly noticed that the train was starting to move.

"Quick, sir! I've got to go!" cried Tom. The man threw some money into his hand and helped Tom gather up his bundles.

"Wait, wait!" Tom shouted.

He ran after the train, with both arms full of heavy stacks of papers. Huffing and puffing, Tom was just able to catch the rear step of a freight car, but he was too loaded down to pull himself on board. "Help!" Tom cried.

A trainman happened to be right there. "Hold on, sonny, I've gotcha!" he said. But with Tom's arms folded tightly around the newspapers, the man pulled the next closest things—Tom's ears!

"I gotcha!" the trainman said again, gripping Tom's ears harder as the train gathered speed. A second later, Tom might have been swept underneath the train's wheels. Instead, the man lifted Tom on board by his ears. But as he did so, Tom suddenly heard a snap inside his head. In a split second, the noise of the train clickety-clacking down the tracks turned into a sound as soft as the hum inside a seashell. Tom shook his head and looked up at the trainman.

"You all right?" the man asked.

"What did you say?" asked Tom. His own voice sounded miles away.

"I asked if you were all right," the man said, louder and more slowly this time.

Tom could hear only a few of the words the man had said, but at least he understood him. "Yes, thank you!" Tom replied.

The trainman had saved Tom's life, but it had cost Tom the better part of his hearing. His childhood illness had made Tom hard of hearing. Now, although he was not completely deaf, Tom could no longer hear ordinary sounds or conversations. One of the things Tom grew to miss most was the simple pleasure of hearing the birds sing.

Oddly enough, Tom could hear people talking softly when the train was at its loudest. The train's whistle would be blowing and people would be shouting to be heard above the engine. At those moments, Tom could hear women telling each other secrets they thought no one else could possibly hear.

Tom went to many doctors to see what could be done to help get his hearing back. Some doctors traced his deafness to the scarlet fever he had had years before. But no doctor was sure of the exact cause, and Tom was never cured.

Once Tom got over the shock of being deaf, or nearly deaf, he accepted his situation. He did not feel particularly sorry for himself, and he did not expect others to feel sorry for him either. With the sounds of everyday life cut out, Tom's world was quiet, allowing him time to think and be alone with himself.

This was different, though, from being alone in his father's observation tower or alone in his basement laboratory. The main difference was that the boyish light-heartedness of Tom's early days was gone. Tom became shy, more solitary and more serious. He realized that he had hardly read or studied at all in his months as a newsboy, and he determined to correct that. He decided that he had to learn everything possible and that he was his own best teacher.

Tom started this new course of action at the reading

room of the Young Men's Association in Detroit. He enjoyed this plunge back into his studies, though it reminded him of how little time he had to spend at home in his laboratory.

One day, after Tom had been a newsboy for more than a year, it occurred to him that the baggage and mail car in the front of the train had a lot of empty space. Tom thought, "Why not set up my laboratory in there?" The conductor, a friendly Scotsman named Alexander Stevenson, gave Tom permission.

Soon all of Tom's bottles, jars, test tubes and batteries were arranged on shelves built along the back wall of the train car. The shelves were specially made to hold the jars and bottles so that they would not fall out as the train bounced along the tracks. Without knowing it, Tom Edison had created the first moving chemical laboratory!

Throughout the year 1861, Tom spent many a happy layover in Detroit working in the Grand Trunk laboratory. He did more experiments with electricity and wet-cell batteries, and he made his first rough telegraph instruments. The more he worked and studied and experimented, the less he missed hearing the noise and what he called the "foolish chatter" of the outside world.

During that year, the newspapers that Tom sold were filled with articles debating whether or not freedom should be given to the black African slaves working on Southern plantations. One banner headline announced that Abraham Lincoln had been elected President of the United States. Meanwhile, the Pony Express service came to an end with the completion of the first telegraph

Tom's first laboratory aboard the train's baggage car.

line across the continent. But at that time, not even a telegraph line could hold the fragile nation together.

By 1861, there were distinct differences between the Northern and Southern ways of life, and each side wanted to be more powerful than the other. Whenever a new territory became a state in the Southern region, the North would worry. The South felt worried when a new state was created in the North.

The main issue dividing the North from the South, through, was slavery. In the South, slavery had been established for nearly one hundred years. The wealthy cotton plantation owners depended on slaves to pick the cotton and do the heavy labor around the huge estates. Though most people in the South were not rich enough to have slaves of their own, they felt that slavery was right for the fortunate few who did have slave labor.

In the North, life was different. Farms were smaller and did not need slave labor; neither did the cities, which were growing at a fast pace. By the shaky year of 1861, slaves were free in the North but not in the South.

To strengthen their position, the Southern states decided to band together to become their own nation. They called themselves the *Confederacy*. In the Confederacy, it would be legal to own slaves. The North, meanwhile, became known as the *Union* or the *Federals*. The Union states thought slavery should be abolished in the South and North forever. Both sides were very angry at each other, and also very nervous, each side waiting for the other to perhaps pull some kind of trick.

One morning, Tom noticed a new headline. It said that the Confederate Army had fired on the Union Army at Fort Sumter, South Carolina. All this was far from Port Huron, and Tom was not exactly sure what it all meant.

What did it mean? The Civil War had begun.

CHAPTER FOUR

Tom's Great Idea

July 22, 1861: DISASTER AT BULL RUN!
Union Troops Slaughtered
Confederates Win War's Biggest Battle
Union: "War May Take Longer Than Anticipated"

Oct. 22, 1861: UNION TROOPS CRUSHED IN
CONFEDERATE AMBUSH
Thousands Fall in Bloody Attack at Ball's Bluff, Va.

Feb. 17, 1862: TRIUMPHANT UNION WINS
FIRST BATTLE
Union Traps Confederates at Ft. Donelson, Tenn.
Gen. Grant Forces Southern Defeat:
Says: "No Terms But Unconditional Surrender"

These headlines appeared on newspapers throughout the North as the Civil War progressed. At the beginning, the Confederate Army seemed to turn every battle into a victory for the South—and a bloodbath for the Union Army of the North. The Southern soldiers thought they would win easily and soon be able to return home and back to their old way of life. The Northern troops, however, were not easily discouraged. Every battle lost meant facing each new one with a full-scale display of force. Though the North did not start winning right away, eventually the tide began to turn.

During that time, Tom worked extra hard to sell newspapers. Each afternoon, Tom put in an order at the Detroit *Free Press* for a certain number of copies, usually around two hundred. He hoped to sell all of these on the train and at the station stops between Detroit and Port Huron. The more newspapers he sold, the better he did. It was often tempting to ask for more newspapers, especially with the news about the war. But if he asked for too many and couldn't sell them all, he would have to pay for the leftovers. For that reason, Tom was having a tough time earning money as a newsboy.

As the war progressed, though, Tom began to notice a pattern. Whenever the *Free Press* contained a particularly strong headline about a recent battle, he not only sold more copies than usual, but he also could barely carry enough copies to the train. Soon, part of his daily afternoon routine was to go down to the Detroit *Free Press* building itself to find out in advance what the new edition's headlines would be. That way, he could better judge how many copies to order.

One afternoon in April 1862, Tom was down at the *Free Press* office when the telegraph suddenly started clattering out a report on a recent battle. The two staff reporters jumped up from their desks to see what the telegraph operator was deciphering.

"Victory for the North!" one of them shouted to the rest of the room.

A cheer went up, and more people crowded around the telegraph operator.

The chief editor frowned as he looked down at the operator's notes. "Sixty thousand believed dead or wounded! I don't call *that* a victory, no matter *who* won," he said, shaking his head. "That must have been an incredible battle."

"General Wallace killed in action!" gasped a secretary.

"Well, looks like the South had two of its big generals killed too," muttered an errand boy.

"But what about my boy! He's out there, too!" cried a reporter's wife, who happened to be in the office. Her husband immediately put his arms around her and walked her out of the room.

"Is General Grant okay?" a printer cried, trying to see over the crowd of heads.

"Nothing definite, but I think he's all right," someone called back.

"C'mon, boys," the editor said, "we gotta make up some headlines." But no one, not even the editor, moved. Everyone was too caught up in the shocking news that was coming over the wire.

Tom also found himself glued to the telegrapher's side. For one thing, he realized he could *hear* the clicking sound of the telegraph, though he could not hear much of the distracting talking and noise around him.

As the afternoon wore on, Tom learned that the day's newspaper would carry a huge banner announcing that

33

60,000 were believed killed or wounded in a three-day battle at Shiloh, Tennessee.

"If only people along the train line could know what happened," Tom thought anxiously. He figured that if other people reacted as the people in the newsroom had, everyone would want to see a newspaper. Suddenly, he had an idea, and he walked over to the telegraph operator.

The weary telegrapher looked up and smiled at the young, enterprising boy beside him. "Hello, Edison," he said. "What can I do for you?"

Gravely, Tom told him his idea: if he could wire the other train stations from Detroit to Port Huron, the telegraphers at each station could chalk the headline on the boards before the train arrived. By the time the train reached each station, the people along the line would be eager for the news and would want to buy a newspaper.

"Well, Edison, you've got an idea there," the operator said slowly. Still, the man looked tired and not entirely sure he wanted to act on Tom's plan.

Tom offered fruit, candy, newspapers, magazine subscriptions—anything—if he would try it.

"Well," he sighed, after thinking a moment, "you've got a deal."

With that, Tom went to the man in charge of newspaper distribution. When he told him the amount he wanted to sell that afternoon, the man scoffed and shooed Tom away. Determined to see his plan through, Tom marched boldly up to William Storey, the *Free Press* managing editor.

"Mr. Storey," Tom said, "I'd like to request one thousand newspapers for this afternoon's order."

"One thousand copies," repeated Mr. Storey sternly. "That's quite a bit more than your usual amount, isn't it, Mr. Edison?"

Tom agreed that it was, but he said he was positive he could sell that many, with the account of the battle and all.

Mr. Storey studied the boy standing squarely before his desk. Despite his shabby appearance, Tom looked sure of what he was doing. "All right," said Mr. Storey, "I'll put you down for a thousand, on credit to the newspaper."

"Thank you, sir!" exclaimed Tom.

Tom's plan worked even better than he expected.

As the train approached the first station out of Detroit, Tom stuck his head out the window. He saw what looked like a large group of people on a day's outing. He reached over and took out six newspapers, four more than his usual amount. He was ready to sell them for five cents apiece. But as the train pulled into the station, he realized the large gathering was not a group, but a crowd waiting for news. People were waving their hands wildly and calling out, "Here! Newsboy! Toss me a paper!"

Tom quickly sold the ones he had in his hand and then rushed back to his bundle and grabbed an armful. When he got back to the platform, he sold forty newspapers at ten cents each!

Mount Clemons was the next station, and when the train came into sight, the crowd of people became a howling mob. Tom usually sold about a dozen newspapers at that station, but that day he sold 150—at fifteen cents apiece!

The scene was the same at each stop along the way. By the time the train reached its final stop at Port Huron, Tom had only a small bundle of papers left. Because the station was a mile from town, Tom shouldered his remaining bundle and started walking. When he was less than halfway to the town center, he saw a large crowd of people hurrying toward the station. Tom smiled to himself, guessing what they wanted. He then looked around and stopped in front of a church, where a prayer meeting was being held.

As the people rushed toward him, Tom called out, "Extra! Extra! Sixty thousand may be dead and wounded in Shiloh battle! Extra! Extra!"

The crowd hardly needed any more advertisement.

"Here, newsboy! Let me have a paper!"

"Sorry, sir. I'll need thirty-five cents."

"Here you go! Let me see it, boy!"

The frantic jingle of change was music to Tom Edison's ears as his newspaper bundle became smaller and smaller. Within two minutes, the prayer meeting had ended and the church doors were flung open. People poured out and headed over to Tom. By the ease with which the churchgoers found thirty-five cents for a paper, it seemed clear to Tom that the minister had not even passed the collection plate yet.

Tom counted his day's earnings that evening and felt quite proud of himself—and also quite wealthy. The

Extra! Extra! 60,000 believed killed or wounded at Shiloh!

posted headlines had made all the difference, he realized. The telegraph was a true marvel! So were newspapers, for that matter. Maybe I'll be a famous telegraph operator! he thought, Or maybe a great reporter! For Tom Edison, the world was suddenly brimming with possibilities for the future. There were so many paths to choose from, he wondered how he would ever decide on only one!

CHAPTER FIVE

Setbacks and A Step Forward

Tom was now fifteen and could not stop thinking about his future. Telegraph operator, reporter and (for a short while) even railroad mechanic were some of the job possibilities Tom considered. Such jobs, he thought, would be interesting enough ways to earn a living and carry on with his experiments in chemistry.

With some of the money he saved from the sale of the Battle of Shiloh paper, Tom was able to buy a small, secondhand printing press, along with three hundred pounds of old metal type from the Detroit *Free Press*. Before long, he had taught himself how to set type and run the press. Not long afterward, Tom set up a newspaper shop in the same train car of the Grand Trunk Railway that held his chemistry lab. In that car, Editor-in-Chief Tom Edison wrote, edited and printed his own local newspaper, *The Weekly Herald*, which he sold for eight cents a copy. Tom's newspaper was the first one in the world to be printed in a train car.

The Weekly Herald, or "Grand Trunk Herald," as it was sometimes called, contained local news and gossip and reported railroad service and changes of schedule. It also reported any births, deaths and retirements, as well as the names of volunteers for war service, that Tom knew about. Sometimes Tom would include odd bits of Civil War news that he received over the telegraph wires before the big newspapers knew about them. Tom's editorial columns discussed many difficult topics, though they sometimes sounded just like the skeptical young Edison.

Many people liked Tom's newspaper, and in time, he had four hundred regular readers. Luckily for Tom, readers did not seem to mind his bad spelling and sometimes peculiar way of writing. For example:

ABOUT TO RETIRE

We were informed that Mr. Eden is about to retire from the Grand Trunk's eating-house and Point Edwards . . . We are shure that he retires with the well wishes of the community at large.

After a while, a friend of Tom's who worked on a Port Huron newspaper persuaded Tom to change the way he wrote his paper.

"Your paper is a nice paper, with a little bit of everything to read," the friend observed. "But if you concentrate on the wealthy local people and personal gossip, why, you'd be making a paper that people would *have* to read, not just simply *like* to read!"

Tom thought the advice over and decided his friend was right. He changed *The Weekly Herald* to the *Paul Pry* and added a large gossip section. This paper also suffered from Tom's bad spelling and awkward sentences, but nobody seemed to mind.

What one reader did mind, however, was an article about himself that included a little too much news. The reader was a prominant figure in Port Huron and was deeply embarrassed by a gossipy article Tom wrote about him. The man was so angry that the next time he saw Tom, he threw the nosy reporter into the cold St. Clair River! Though Tom was a good swimmer and was not hurt, the surprise plunge was enough to dampen Tom's desire to put out any more newspapers at all. The Grand Trunk Railway newsroom was quickly closed for good.

Once again the train car was just a chemistry lab, and Tom turned his interest back to his experiments. Unfortunately, the conductor, Mr. Stevenson, was growing tired of Tom's chemistry lab and the strange, horrible smells that sometimes came from it. Passengers would complain to him about the smell, so he would have to ask Tom to change his experiments. To Mr. Stevenson, Tom's chemistry lab was nothing but trouble.

One day, as the train rattled and bobbed its way from station to station, shaking the jars of chemicals as it went, Tom did not notice that a cork had popped out of a bottle of phosphorus. That particular chemical is a highly poisonous one that has quick reactions in experiments. Even in Tom's day, phosphorus was used in fireworks and firearms.

When the train lurched to a stop at the next station,

the bottle was thrown out of the rack and onto the car floor. Tom whirled around to find out what had fallen.

"Oh, no—fire!" he cried, quickly stomping on the flames with his foot. Though the fire was easily extinguished, the floor was scorched and the phosphorus's terrible smell was sure to find its way to Mr. Stevenson's nose.

"Edison!" The conductor's voice boomed as he approached the car. "Now, what—" Mr. Stevenson stopped as he saw the burnt wooden floor.

"Let me explain, sir! It was an accident!" Tom began.

"There can be no more accidents, no more experiments! This is the last straw, Edison!" shouted the angry conductor.

With that, he took Tom by the collar and threw him off the train. Then Tom watched in horror as Mr. Stevenson pitched his entire chemistry lab off the train; Tom's beloved chemical jars, experiments and equipment were suddenly raining down upon him.

As the train pulled out of the station and out of sight, there was hardly a more forlorn creature to be found than Tom Edison. The old, battered railway car laboratory, with all Tom's primitive equipment, was dearer to him than the most expensive, modern laboratory of a successful scientist. The sudden loss of it all was a shock to Tom.

Nevertheless, Tom found there was nothing to do but accept the situation and move on. He did not lose his job as trainboy; but after that incident, Tom had to keep his experiments in his father's basement in Port Huron.

It was then that Tom bought a book on telegraphy. With his dreams of being a reporter dashed, Tom turned back to learning about the telegraph machine. By watching the telegraph operators at the railway stations and studying their machines, Tom was able to build his own telegraph machine. This one was an improvement over the one he had made a few years before.

This time, Tom set up a longer telegraph wire. Using stovepipe wire again, he ran it about a half-mile, stringing it over tree branches, to the home of his friend, James Clancy.

Though Tom usually arrived home from work after ten o'clock at night, he would always eagerly stay up and practice sending and receiving messages with his pal, James. This was Tom's way of having fun at the end of a long day. At first, Mr. Edison did not approve of Tom's late-night "playing." He thought that Tom should go to bed. But soon Tom found a way of convincing his father that he should stay up with his telegraph instead.

Tom had noticed that his father liked to read one of the extra newspapers that he usually brought home with him at the end of the day. One night, Tom tried an experiment with his father. He did not bring home any extra newspapers at all.

"No newspapers tonight, son?" asked Mr. Edison, as Tom started to head downstairs to his telegraph.

"Nope," said Tom, stopping at the top of the stairs. "Business was great today!"

Mr. Edison frowned, disappointed at not being able

to know the news. Tom caught his father's look and smiled inside.

"I've got an idea!" Tom exclaimed, as if he had just thought of it. "James Clancy's parents get a newspaper every day. I bet I could get Clancy to telegraph the main news stories over our wire."

Mr. Edison brightened. "Really?" he asked. "Why don't you try it then and see how it works."

For that night and many nights afterward, Mr. Edison allowed his son to stay up until midnight, or even later. Tom would practice the Morse code and receive news over the telegraph wire. Tom's father never suspected the real reason for the sudden "increase" in the newspaper business. Still, he was happy to get the news somehow. Tom was particularly pleased that his plan had worked. Now he could stay up, he could also learn telegraphy without being bothered. This ended suddenly, however. One night, a cow happened to wander through the orchard. Unaware of Tom's telegraph line, the poor cow tripped over a low section of wire and brought the whole line down.

Little did Tom know then that his days as a real telegraph operator were not far away.

Late in the summer of 1862, the Grand Trunk Railway pulled into the Mt. Clemons station. There was a delay there while Tom's train helped push a derailed boxcar back onto the track. Tom watched the process from the platform, holding a bundle of newspapers under his arm.

Spotting the friendly stationmaster, he called out,

"Hello, Mr. Mackenzie!" The stationmaster waved back. Tom liked Mr. Mackenzie and, during delays like this, had often stopped to chat with him and play with his three-year-old son, Jimmy.

As Tom looked around for little Jimmy Mackenzie, he noticed that the boxcar was finally back on track, sliding down toward the station. Suddenly, Tom saw something that horrified him. Jimmy was sitting on the very track along which the boxcar was swiftly rolling. Without hesitating, Tom dropped his newspapers and charged toward the track, scooping up the child in his arms. As the boxcar whooshed past them a split second later, Tom, with Jimmy in his arms, fell onto the other side of the tracks. They were cut and scraped—but they were safe!

"Mr. Mackenzie, come quick!" a railway worker called out.

Mr. Mackenzie came running. Tom handed him his baby while the workers around him explained what had happened—or had almost happened. The stationmaster, holding Jimmy in his arms, was deeply touched and grateful. He wanted to reward Tom in some way, but he did not have much money. However, Mr. Mackenzie had noticed how Tom often hung over his telegraph machine in his effort to learn how to operate it.

"I'll tell you what," said Mr. Mackenzie, "if you'll stop off here four days a week and keep Jimmy out of harm's way, I'll teach you the telegraph."

"You will?" Tom exclaimed, leaping at the idea. But suddenly he thought of just one problem. "What about my newspaper route?" he asked.

Tom rescues the stationmaster's son.

Mr. Mackenzie suggested that Tom could easily get someone to take his place for the few stations between Mt. Clemons and Detroit. He pointed out that most of Tom's earnings came from the stations between Mt. Clemons and Port Huron anyway. Tom knew this was true and was thrilled at the idea.

"I can teach you how to telegraph and prepare you for a job as a night operator," said Mr. Mackenzie. Then he invited Tom to board with him and his family for a few months, paying only for the cost of his food. Meanwhile, Tom could take lessons in telegraphy every night and assist the train dispatcher.

"It's a bargain!" Tom cheered.

CHAPTER SIX

Tom the Wandering Telegrapher

"How exactly does a telegraph work?"

Tom had asked this question to telegraph operators many times during his years as a telegrapher. Though lots of people could work a telegraph, it seemed no one could come up with a good explanation of *how* it worked. The best answer Tom ever got was from a Scottish telegraph repairman:

"If you had a dog like a dachsund that was long enough to reach from Edinburgh to London," the Scotsman replied, "if you pulled his tail in Edinburgh, he would bark in London."

That was simple to understand. But Tom later wrote that he never could completely grasp what went through the dog.

Nevertheless, Tom learned the telegraphy trade eagerly and rapidly in the five months he spent with Mr. Mackenzie. By the time Tom started his study, he was more than ready to learn. In fact, Tom surprised Mr.

Mackenzie when he showed up the first day with his own good set of telegraph instruments, which he had made himself in a gunsmith's shop in Detroit.

The stationmaster saw quickly that his new student was particularly patient and skillful with his hands. Mr. Mackenzie also recognized Tom's clearly inventive mind. Tom was forever finding discarded scraps of wire or metal and thinking of ways to use them.

Once, Tom found a pile of broken-up and corroded battery cells and got permission to strip them. Doing so, he discovered that the cells contained several ounces of sheet platinum. Tom was thrilled. He could use platinum in many experiments. In fact, he used this platinum over and over for many years.

At Mt. Clemons, Tom was trained to send and receive dispatches, and he learned the railroad telegraphers' shortened form of signals. Mr. Mackenzie said that with that knowledge, Tom would be able to get a job as a second-class telegrapher; to become a first-class telegrapher, Tom needed more work and experience. Soon, he got just that.

These were the Civil War years, and telegraphers of all classes were needed everywhere. Telegraph operators not only sent war reports to newspapers but also wired and delivered urgent messages to and from cities, towns and even battlefields.

Telegraph operators were mostly young, single men who were always on the lookout for a better telegraph job somewhere else. There were plenty of jobs to be had. In 1856, there were 132 Western Union telegraph offices;

by 1866, there were 4,000. Even so, none of the jobs paid well. The moment a better opportunity arose somewhere else, the telegrapher would throw his few belongings together and hop on the next train to a new job in another part of the country.

In that way, Tom's experience was typical of the work patterns of other telegraphers. Between 1863 and 1866, Tom worked in at least eight different places, including Port Huron, Michigan; Stratford Junction, Ontario, Canada; Indianapolis, Indiana; Cincinnati, Ohio; and Louisville, Kentucky. The offices he worked in were old and musty, and in some cases plaster fell from the ceiling. Like other young men his age, Tom moved and lived away from home. But with his meager pay, he could only afford rooms at rundown boarding houses, usually not far from where he put in long hours at work.

What made sixteen-year-old Tom different from the other telegraphers? Both what he did when he was not working and how he spent his money. Many telegraphers were rowdy and carefree; they spent their extra money on whisky and beer, and their free time drinking and making merry. They could not understand Tom Edison. In a single afternoon, he could spend half a month's pay on a copper coil and an assortment of wire, batteries, tools, books and other seemingly worthless junk. But to Tom, the things he was collecting were worth much more than his monthly salary. He was happy to give up food and clothing to buy them, and he willingly gave up sleep to experiment with them.

From the start of his telegrapher days, Tom followed

his natural impulse to experiment and tinker. Before long, he put this talent to work for him. At his second job, in Stratford Junction, Tom worked from seven in the evening until seven in the morning. Since train traffic was light at those times, Tom was content to read or work on some experimental mechanical device. Sometimes he took little naps at those hours to make up for the sleep he skipped while reading or experimenting during the day.

While on duty, though, Tom was supposed to send a signal over the wire at certain hours to let the train dispatcher know that he was still paying attention to his job. As time passed, the train dispatcher noticed that Tom always signaled in on time but he never seemed to answer any messages after that. When the dispatcher investigated the reason for this one night, he found that Tom had devised a way of making the telegraph automatically send the signal over the wire. Meanwhile, Tom was blissfully asleep in his chair! When the railroad officials found out, they were not amused, despite Tom's show of inventiveness.

In fact, more often than not, Tom's experiments and electrical devices were not appreciated by his employers. For one thing, Tom often neglected his telegraph work if he happened to be working on something of his own. Sometimes, Tom would even stop the telegraph operator from sending a message so that he could quickly write down an idea that had just come to him. When he was finished writing, he would signal the operator to continue.

Still, Tom was becoming more and more skilled as a telegrapher. When he put his mind to it, he could receive messages with lightning-like speed. But in the end, Tom was fired from many of his jobs for two reasons: he did not like to take orders from his boss, and he often paid more attention to his own experiments than he did to his work. Getting fired did not seem to bother Tom, for he always found another job.

Tom's employer at the telegraph office in Cincinnati was impressed by how quickly and well Tom could take down messages. He promoted Tom to first-class operator, at the seemingly enormous salary of a hundred and five dollars a month! The work in that office was fast and grueling—like running up a steep hill all day long. The fast operators, like Tom, sent messages at the top speed of forty-five words a minute. The responses often came back in such a tight, shortened form that the operators merely wrote down the messages without thinking about what they meant.

April 14, 1865, was an especially busy day in the office. None of the operators knew why, until someone happened to notice a large crowd around the Cincinnati *Enquirer* newspaper office. Clearly, something had made news. A messenger went down and brought back a newspaper with the shocking headline: "LINCOLN SHOT."

The telegraphers not only were surprised but also wondered how they could not have known President Abraham Lincoln had been shot when they were the ones passing the news on to the newspaper. They all immediately went through every message they had copied down that day. It turned out that one young man in the office had copied down the message. Yet, as Tom later recalled, the man had worked so mechanically that he had copied it without having the slightest idea of what it meant.

Tom made a friend in the Cincinnati office named Milton Adams. As friends, the two could not have been more different. Milton was carefree and playful, and he dressed in sharp, snappy outfits. Tom, on the other hand, was more of a loner who did not fit in with the others. Tom wore baggy shirts and pants, topped off with a straw hat. That, along with his thin face, and hair that would not stay in place, made him look like a country hick.

But Milton liked Tom and was amused by his strange ways and ideas. He remembered one of Tom's first inventions: a rattrap. The boarding house in which Tom lived was so filled with rats that Tom decided to do something about it. He took two metal plates and insulated them from each other. Then he connected them with a main battery. When a rat happened to put its front feet on one plate and its back feet on the other—ZAP! The rat would be no more.

By the time Tom arrived at his new job in Louisville, he was no longer just interested in doing odd experiments. He wanted to invent! Tom started up his self-education once again. He bought stacks of old science magazines and twenty volumes of a particular book of general knowledge. He even tried to teach himself a foreign language.

During that time, Tom also taught himself a different

way of writing. He stopped printing letters the fancy, curvy way he had been taught and started writing as simply as he could. His new way, he found, was a big timesaver.

In Louisville, Tom became interested in a new way to telegraph. He wanted to have one message going out over the wire and one coming in at the same time. Such a device would be called a duplex telegraph. It could cut in half the cost and time it took to send two messages. Though he had thought about such an invention before, this time Tom hoped to find the solution. He worked days and nights on this scheme.

One day, Tom took apart all the telegraph instruments and rewired them—with no result. The office manager was quite annoyed at what Tom had done and refused to let Tom work with the circuits and batteries after that. This frustrated Tom. But being so curious and so determined to invent the duplex, he went against the manager's order. This only brought more trouble.

"I went one night to the battery room to obtain some sulfuric acid for experimenting," Tom remembered years later. Unfortunately, he accidentally tipped over a glass bottle that was used to hold special acidic liquids; these liquids were so acidic that they could dissolve other materials.

"The acid ran out of the bottle," Tom later explained. "It went through the ceiling to the manager's room below, and ate up his desk and all the carpet. The next morning I was summoned before him and told that the company wanted operators, not experimenters."

Tom was sorry about that incident, especially because no one in the office trusted him after that. This was particularly hard on Tom because he felt so close to the answer. All he needed, he felt sure, was a hundred dollars or so to complete the structure he had been building. But no one would lend him any money.

A short time later, an inventor from Boston, J. B. Stearns, came up with the duplex machine himself. Stearns received a patent from the U.S. government on his invention, which certified that the invention was his and only his. Tom was crushed.

But Tom's desire to invent still burned inside him. Not only would he try to make a better duplex telegraph, but he had a rough idea for a machine that could take three, maybe even four messages at the same time. The trouble was, Tom needed equipment, money and time to work on his ideas, and he had so little of all of those.

At times, Tom felt that he would never succeed at anything. Once, he even thought of sailing to South America and seeking his fortune there. Instead, Tom went home to Port Huron to rest, only to find that his parents were being forced to leave their home. The military had changed command and was taking over the Edison house. This upset Mrs. Edison so much that she became ill and did not act like herself. Mr. Edison started staying away from home more and more to avoid her.

Feeling uncomfortable at home, Tom soon wanted to tackle a new job in a new place, like the East Coast. A friend told about an opening in the Boston office of Western Union. Boston! To Tom, that city was the nation's center of culture and scientific learning. Boston was also the home of Yankee inventors, like J. B. Stearns. There were also several well-established manufacturers of fine electrical equipment in Boston. There, he might find people he could talk to and learn from—perhaps he could even find the answers to some of his many questions.

On the train headed a thousand miles due east, Tom felt his dreams were just within reach. The more he thought about it, the more he was sure Boston was just the place for a young, aspiring inventor!

CHAPTER SEVEN

Inventions and Failures

The train trip to Boston was slow and cold, but it finally ended. Tom headed straight for the Western Union office to apply for a job. As Tom walked into the office, heads began to turn.

"Who's this from the wild, woolly West?" one telegrapher murmured to another.

Tom was not blind to the curious looks on the faces of the office workers. He knew he looked rumpled from four days on the train. He also knew that he did not care to dress as freshly or stylishly as the Eastern telegraph operators. So he just let them laugh.

Getting the job was easy. Tom showed the manager copies of transcripts made in his neat, new handwriting and letters from former employers vouching for his speed and accuracy. After a five-minute interview, Tom was hired.

The day's real hurdle lay ahead. He had to rise to the "secret little joke" his co-workers played on him. They had him take down messages from the fastest operator in the East, who was based in New York. Tom could tell a joke was being played on him by the smirks on his co-workers' faces. But he pretended not to notice. Tom worked just as fast as the operator from New York. He even paused to sharpen his pencil, just to let his co-workers know he was not worried. When the New York operator started to wear out, Tom sent a message back that said, "Say, young man, change off and send with the other foot!" With that, the New York operator quit the game, and Tom won his office's respect.

In Boston, Tom met up with his old Cincinnati pal, Milton Adams. Together, they roomed in a boarding house on Exeter Street. Soon, their room became crowded with books, chemicals and assorted wires and metals that Tom had picked up in the city's shops and junkyards.

One of Tom's most important discoveries was a secondhand copy of Michael Faraday's two-volume work, *Experimental Researches in Electricity*. Tom later claimed that the book changed his life. Michael Faraday was a great English scientist who had spent much of his life researching and doing experiments in Tom's favorite field, electricity. Reading over Faraday's experiments gave Tom hope that he, too, could one day understand electricity and invent something from it—something that had never been made before.

Tom began reading Faraday's book at four o'clock in the morning, when he arrived home from work. Tom could not put the book down. When his roommate, Milton, arrived back from his day shift, he was surprised to find Tom still reading the same book.

"Good book?" Milton asked, knowing full well what kind of book it was.

"Adams," said Tom, shutting the book. He jumped up and started getting ready for work. "I am now twenty-one. I may live to be fifty. Can I get as much done as he did?" Tom wondered aloud, pointing to Faraday's book. "I have got so much to do and life is so short, I am going to hustle!" With that, Tom dashed off to work.

At the Boston Western Union office, Tom worked the night shift. His routine there was much like his other jobs. That is, he did his telegraph work whenever the chief operator angrily reminded him of the job. Tom spent the rest of the time dreaming of inventions and drawing diagrams to suit them.

During the day, when Tom was not collecting odds and ends, he visited shops in which some of the country's finest scientific minds were at work. There was Charles Williams Jr.'s shop on Court Street, where skilled men worked on telegraphic and other fine electrical instruments. (A year or two later, another aspiring, but unknown, inventor would work there—a man named Alexander Graham Bell, who was working on what he called a speaking telegraph.) There was Thomas Hall's shop, which had produced miniature electric trains when Tom was a boy. Tom even visited the first duplex maker, J. B. Stearns. These men enjoyed talking with Tom, for they appreciated his fine mind and interest in their work. To Tom, being around them was terrifically exciting and gave him many ideas.

At that time, Tom was working hard to come up

with a better duplex telegraph machine than the one Stearns had invented. Tom felt that making his own duplex machine was the most important step he could take right then.

At last, in June 1868, a little article appeared in a telegraph trade magazine. It said, "Mr. Thomas A. Edison, of the Western Union Office, Boston," had invented a type of telegraph that carried messages both ways on a single wire. The article, which Tom helped his friend, Milton Adams, write, called the invention "interesting, simple and ingenious."

But no matter who had written the article, the fact was that it received much attention. A few men even came to Tom and gave him money so that he could keep on experimenting. (The kind of money Tom received is called capital, and the men who gave it to him are investors, or financial backers. Capital is different from a reward or any other kind of monetary gift. It must be spent for a specific purpose—in Tom's case, on his inventions.)

By that time, Tom had been a telegrapher for more than six years. He was more than tired of this kind of work. For years, he had felt like a slave, working long, dreary hours for little pay. When Tom received the capital from the investors, he decided to quit his job and start on his own as an inventor. He would be his own boss, and people would pay him for his inventions. Never again would Tom have to be interrupted while working on a project. The idea excited him.

Tom soon set up a lab at Charles William's shop on Court Street. He put notices and advertisements in magazines, stating his address and his experience as an inventor and informing people that models of his duplex machine were for sale at four hundred dollars.

Within six months, Tom had several projects going at once. He had also received small amounts of capital from three more investors. One of the projects was a telegraphic vote-recording machine. It was a simple, but bulky, invention that could record votes from an audience, or from representatives and senators, by using telegraphic power. The vote recorder was Tom's first real invention, and he received a U.S. Government patent on it on June 1, 1869.

Tom was thrilled with his first invention. Using the knowledge he acquired by studying the telegraph, he had dreamed up the vote recorder himself. As a telegrapher waiting to send out news to Congress, Tom had noticed how long it took the senators and representatives to call in their votes. Tom imagined that Congress would be delighted with his timesaving vote recorder.

How wrong Tom was!

"It's no use," said a man at the Massachusetts legislature.

"Impossible!" Tom exclaimed, horrified. "I know it will work!"

"Yes," replied the man, "for that very reason it is a failure. I talked with some of the members and they explained why." The man said that as things stood, all views could be heard before a vote was tallied. Any representatives who disagreed with the main opinion could get up and speak while a vote was taking place. He could try

Tom beside his first patented invention, the electrical vote recorder.

to persuade others to his point of view. A vote recorder, since it worked so quickly, would take away that opportunity.

"In short," said the man, "the legislature would not have your invention if you paid them to use it."

Tom was disappointed, but not discouraged. He took his invention to Washington, D.C.—only to receive a similar reply from someone else.

This time, Tom realized that the vote recorder was no good. He resolved never to make another useless invention. From that day onward, Tom always made sure of the need for an invention before deciding to make it. This simple idea—trying to learn first what the public wanted—was part of Edison's genius.

Though his vote recorder had failed, Tom was eager to conduct a large-scale trial of his duplex telegraph. His machine was not too different from J. B. Stearn's telegraph, but he received some five hundred dollars of capital for it anyway. Investors probably felt that Tom could come up with improvements in time and speed.

His first major experiment to test his duplex telegraph was set up with the Atlantic & Pacific Telegraph Company in Rochester, New York. The company invited Tom to come and string his telegraph wires between Rochester and New York City, some four hundred miles apart.

To do this, Tom got a loan from a friend for eight hundred dollars. This was a lot of money, but Tom was fairly sure his new machine would work. He took his equipment to Rochester, leaving the New York operator with a complete list of instructions.

He arrived in Rochester on a Saturday and waited until the early morning hours of Sunday, when the lines between Rochester and New York City would be entirely clear. Then Tom began to telegraph. Click, click, click . . .

Nothing happened. Edison signaled and signaled, but he could get no response from New York at all. He decided that the operator there either had failed to do his part or could not understand the instructions. On the other hand, the trouble may have been in the wiring. Tom tried his experiment several more times that week, still without success. Finally, Tom gave up and went back to Boston.

This time, Tom was in a tight spot. He owed eight hundred dollars to the man who had loaned him the money for the duplex experiment. Tom had no money, and two failed inventions to his name. He saw no way that any more people would want to invest in his work. As far as Tom was concerned, his future was ruined in Boston.

Tom thought it would be a good idea to go to another, larger city where he was not known. Perhaps he would have better luck in the next place. With that, he borrowed a few dollars from a telegrapher friend, set off on a boat for New York City and arrived the next morning. He stepped off the ship not knowing a soul, with nowhere to stay and without a cent to his name.

CHAPTER EIGHT

From Rags to Riches

I n 1869, New York was bustling with the energy of a large and growing city. As Tom wandered slowly away from the busy docks on that warm spring morning, his eyes were wide open with all there was to see.

Such Traffic! Why, there were horse-drawn carts and carriages everywhere he looked. Men in starched black coats and top hats were calling out orders to their horses and yelling to any cart or person who got in the way. Women in shawls carried baskets of food and called to their children to stay next to them. He passed store after store after store, filled with every imaginable kind of goods.

Soon Tom came to a large market area. There, whole sides of cows were carried to packing houses on trains that ran on tracks two stories above the ground! On the cobblestone streets rolled hundreds of carts filled with fruits, poultry, dairy products and vegetables for sale. Boston was a big city, but even at just a first glance, New York already seemed much, much bigger. Much noisier, too.

But for Tom, who could not hear much of the noise about him, the worst sound of the moment came from his stomach. He was hungry, as hungry as he could possibly be. Walking along, seeing all that food and knowing he had no money, Tom's hunger pangs sounded even louder.

Tom turned down a side street, and looked through the window of a wholesale tea house. He saw a tea salesman urging a customer to buy a certain tea. The customer looked unsure, so the salesman gave him a free sample to try at home. After a few more minutes, the customer walked away and Tom went inside.

"Good morning, kid, how can I help you?" asked the tea salesman. Though Tom was twenty-two years old, he looked much younger in his baggy, careless clothes and straw hat.

"I'd like a sample bag of your tea, so I might take it home and try if for myself," replied Tom.

"Sure," said the man, and handed Tom a small bag of tea.

By the end of that morning, Tom had eaten a meal he would never forget at a well-known downtown restaurant. There, he had managed to exchange his packet of tea for a baked apple dumpling and a cup of coffee. The size of the meal had not mattered to Tom. It had tasted so good on his empty stomach that apple dumplings remained his favorite dish for the rest of his life.

Now that his hunger was out of the way, Tom could think about more important things—like where he would sleep that night and what he might do for money. He thought of all the people he knew and remembered one old telegrapher friend who lived in New York City. Perhaps he could let Tom have a space on his floor, or even lend him some money, until he found a job. After many enquiries, Tom finally got his friend's address and walked uptown to his apartment.

"He's not home!" a neighbor shouted, annoyed at Tom's persistent knocks.

"Do you know when he'll be back?" asked Tom.

"No idea. Maybe tomorrow, maybe next week," came the answer.

Tom spent his first night in New York walking the streets until dawn. Though he hoped he would not have to do the same the next night, he had expected this might happen. But Tom was used to being in difficult situations. He felt sure something would turn up. And soon enough, his luck changed for the better.

First, Tom ran across a telegrapher friend whom he had not expected to see. Though his friend was also out of a job and could lend Tom only a dollar, that dollar, to Tom, was a lot better than nothing. Next, he called upon Franklin L. Pope, an electrical engineer and telegraph expert whom Tom had heard of while in Boston.

Pope, Tom found out, worked at the Gold Indicator Company, in the city's financial district. In that district were many banks, stock brokerage firms and other businesses where shares of gold and stock were the main items being bought and sold.

Tom did not know anything about stock and gold. Nor was he interested in knowing how millions of dollars were traded on the stock and gold markets every day. What mattered to Tom were two recent inventions that had brought both the gold and the stock market businesses one giant step forward.

The first of these devices, invented by Dr. S. S. Laws, was a gold indicator. This machine was similar to the telegraph, for it sent messages over a wire; but rather than telling news, it told the latest prices for buying or selling gold. The following year, a man named E. A. Callahan had improved upon the gold indicator. He added a little electrical type wheel, which made a ticking sound. His machine could send gold and stock market prices by wire and then print them onto a moving paper tape. Callahan called his machine a stock ticker.

Tom had studied Callahan's stock ticker while in Boston and had made several improvements on it. These improvements were good enough for Tom to receive a patent on them. He also earned some money from an investor. Before Tom left Boston, a company had bought Tom's stock ticker and had gotten thirty businesses to pay for its services.

For that reason, Franklin L. Pope, of the Gold Indicator Company, was happily surprised to see Thomas Edison standing in his office. Franklin, who was just a few years older than Tom, had heard of the young electrical whiz from Boston.

"Why don't you make my office your temporary headquarters?" Franklin suggested. "You could work on your experiments in the company's machine shop."

"Gosh, thanks, but—"

Edison's original phonograph (left) and his universal stock printer of 1871.

"Better than that," Franklin interrupted excitedly, "you could help me with what I'm working on—that is, until you find a job. You see, I'm in charge of making improvements on the central transmitter of the Laws gold indicator. Having you working on it too would be great! That is, until you find a job." Franklin added that last sentence so that he wouldn't sound as though he were pushing Tom into something he did not want to do.

Tom, however, thought it was a fine idea and readily agreed. "The only problem," Tom added, feeling a bit awkward, "is that, well, if I watch my diet closely, I can make my dollar for food last a few days. But do you know where I could sleep in the meantime?"

"Hmmm. Yes, I know!" said Franklin. "There's a cot in the company's battery room, in the cellar of the Mills Building on Broad Street. I'm sure no one would mind if you slept there."

During the next few days, Tom lived happily on five-cent meals of apple dumplings and coffee and studied the Laws gold indicator. Lying on his cot at night, Edison could hardly imagine the millions of dollars that were traded, bought, and sold on the floor above him every day.

Tom had been at the Gold Indicator Company a week or so when one day the whole central transmitting instrument came crashing to a halt. Franklin, who was nearby, rushed to see what was wrong. Even Dr. Laws himself burst from his office.

"What in tarnation is going on?" he bellowed. "Pope! Fix it, immediately!"

"I'm trying, sir! But I don't see anything wrong."

Dr. Laws kept on shouting as he bent over the transmitter with Franklin. But the two men were in such a panic that neither of them were any help at all. If the machine did not start up again quickly, the company's three hundred business clients throughout the city were going to be awfully upset.

Within five minutes, each of the three hundred customer offices had dispatched a messenger to find out what the problem was. Soon, three hundred messengers were shouting and jostling each other outside the Gold Indicator Company building, trying to fight their way in.

"Somebody get rid of those boys!" shouted Dr. Laws. "Pope, you fix this thing or else!"

"Sir, I can't do anything with you shouting in my ear!" Franklin shouted back.

Dr. Laws was beside himself. "If you think I've spent

my life building up this business only to meet ruin with these few minutes, you've—"

Just then, Tom calmly tried to say something to both men. "Excuse me. Excuse me, I think I've found the trouble."

The two men stopped shouting at each other long enough to let Tom's statement sink in. They fixed their eyes on him.

"You see," said Tom, "it seems one of the contact springs has broken off and dropped between two wheels, which has stopped the whole machine."

"Fix it! Fix it! And be quick, for Heaven's sake!" Dr. Laws yelled.

Almost as quickly and easily as the machine had broken down, Tom fixed it. Before long, peace reigned once again at the Gold Indicator Company and for its clients. At that point Dr. Laws, having calmed down, asked Franklin about the young stranger who had so miraculously fixed the transmitter. Franklin told him about Tom—and also said Tom was looking for a job.

Tom's immediate future was settled that afternoon. He would stay on at the company to assist Franklin and would be paid the largest salary he had ever received. The two worked well together and became good friends. But that July, Franklin left Dr. Law's company to go into business for himself. Tom took Franklin's place—at the tremendous salary of three hundred dollars a month!

That summer at the Gold Indicator Company was a busy and productive one for Tom. He continued to work on, improve and receive patents for his telegraph, which was now able to print messages at the other end, not just relay a code.

Tom also improved the Laws gold indicator so that it, like Callahan's stock ticker, could offer a full stock-quotation service along with the gold price changes. The two machines were now equal.

Callahan's company had already been bought out by Western Union, which was the nation's largest telegraph company. Western Union did not like having a full-scale rival on its hands, so it offered to buy Dr. Laws's business from him. Dr. Laws did not want to compete with Western Union, so he agreed to sell the Gold Indicator Company. Dr. Laws retired a wealthy man.

Meanwhile, Tom was offered a job with Western Union. But having been an employee of Western Union for six years already, Tom did not want to go back to that. Instead, he and Franklin went into business together. They set up an electrical engineering service called Pope, Edison & Company—the first one ever in the United States. The "Company" part of the name was a silent partner, the publisher of a telegraph journal, who donated advertising space instead of money. Any money the company made would be split three ways.

The trouble was, Tom did all the work. Through the fall and winter, Tom worked almost without stopping in a small, cold shop in New Jersey. What he made was a new type of printing telegraph called a gold printer. This machine was rented to businesspeople who imported goods or dealt in different currencies. Tom's company rented the service at a much lower rate than Western

Union's and threatened to cut into Western Union's business. Within six months, Western Union had bought Tom's gold printer for fifteen thousand dollars. This pleased Tom immensely, but it bothered him that his two partners had made the same amount without doing any work for it.

In June 1870, Tom resigned from the partnership and once again struck out on his own. When the head of Western Union, General Marshall Lefferts, found out that Tom was working for himself, he proposed a deal: Tom could work independently on improving Western Union's system, and he would be paid separately for each improvement. Tom agreed to this, even though he did not know just how much he would be getting paid.

After Tom turned in a series of minor inventions, General Lefferts asked him to work on the biggest problem in Western Union's system. It was a problem that nearly all machines at the time had: at certain times, the printer would start running wild and printing crazy figures.

In about three weeks, Tom returned to General Lefferts's office with the improvement. He demonstrated it before General Lefferts and the company's board of directors. Tom's improvement was so good, so much better than anyone had imagined, that it made all other current machines seem outdated.

At that point, Tom had not yet received payment for any of his inventions or improvements. General Lefferts knew, with this latest improvement, that it was time to pay Tom for his efforts.

"Well, young man," said the general, "the committee would like to settle up the account for all you've done. How much do you think your work is worth?"

Tom did not know what to say. He so rarely put a price tag on his work. In the back of his mind, he thought he should ask for five thousand dollars. But five thousand dollars! He thought the general would never agree to that. Tom thought he would be happy with three thousand, but he couldn't bring himself to say the figure. Instead, Tom said, "General, suppose you make me an offer."

"All right," said General Lefferts, "how would forty thousand dollars strike you?"

CHAPTER NINE

Tom Sets Up Shop

orty thousand dollars!

Tom clutched the table beside him to keep from falling over in shock. At the same time, he tried to appear casual, as if he had expected to receive forty thousand dollars for his inventions. General Lefferts was still waiting for an answer to his offer.

"I-I th-think your figure sounds fair enough," Tom managed to reply.

A few days later, Tom signed a contract with Western Union, and then he stood holding a check in his hands. He could hardly believe his eyes—a check with his name on it, along with that enormous amount of money. This was the first check Tom had ever received.

I must be dreaming, Tom said to himself. Or worse, he thought, it could all be a practical joke. Why, he had never even been inside a bank before!

But Tom went down to the bank that day to cash his check. Nervously, he stepped up to the bank teller.

"I need to see some identification," the teller said.

"What?" asked Tom. His deafness kept him from hearing what was said; and because it was his first time to a bank, he had no idea what the teller might be saying.

"I need some identification!" the teller repeated, this

time loudly. "I need to verify that you are the same person the check is made out to," he yelled.

Tom could not understand a word the teller was saying. Confused, and now sure that this whole thing had been a trick, he took the check back and sadly returned to the Western Union office. The secretaries at the office giggled when Tom returned empty-handed, which only confirmed Tom's fears of being tricked.

However, once Tom explained what had happened, General Leffert's secretary accompanied him to the bank and cleared up the problem. The money was quickly handed over to Tom in a stack of bills a foot high!

Tom found it extremely awkward carrying that much money back to his house, and once it was there, he was terrified someone would break in and rob him. The next day, a friend suggested that Tom take the money to the bank and open up a bank account. This seemed like a sensible idea to Tom. He was fascinated, too, with the little book he received afterward, which told him how much money he had in the bank.

Tom Edison, who could think of so many complex, scientific ideas and inventions, never did have much business sense. He only knew that money was necessary for him to do his work. The less he dealt with it, he thought, the better.

But along with the forty thousand dollars, Tom had earned himself a chance to set up his own shop, where he could manufacture more stock tickers and work on other projects. In the winter of 1871, Tom rented the top floor of an old three-story building in Newark, New Jersey. This industrial city lay just across the Hudson River from New York.

Though Tom was the head of his shop, Western Union was still partly responsible for his future. After all, the company had given Tom's new business an order for 1,200 stock tickers. This order alone, which was to be fulfilled over several years, was worth nearly half a million dollars. So when Tom left for Newark, Western Union made sure that Tom had a business partner. For that reason, Tom's company was called Edison & Unger, after General Leffert's own business associate, William Unger. But Tom did not let this arrangement bother him. He was happy just to work where he could do the things he liked best.

Within one month of receiving the check for forty thousand dollars, Tom had spent all the money on equipment for his new shop. Still, he had high hopes and prospects that more money would be coming to him. He wrote his parents that winter, proudly telling them of the recent events, and saying that he would be able to send them as much money as they needed.

Though there was not time to go home to Port Huron for a visit, Tom still thought of his mother often. As he frequently said, "She was the making of me." Now that Tom was becoming successful, he wanted to show his mother that her early faith in him had been right all along; and he wanted to thank her for that. But Tom never got the chance. Mrs. Edison died that April.

After his mother's funeral, Tom rushed back to Newark and plunged into his work. As foreman at Edison

Edison reviews drawings with staff members.

& Unger, he hired fifty men to manufacture stock tickers. Because electric machines were still so new, the men he hired were mostly trained as clockmakers and machinists. All were highly skilled craftsmen, accustomed to assembling different mechanisms with their hands.

Among those fifty men, five made up the original core of Tom's staff and would work with Tom for most of their lives. John Ott so impressed Tom with his skill at their first meeting that he became assistant foreman. Another remarkable mechanic and draftsman was Charles Batchelor, a young, friendly Englishman with a black beard. John Kruesi, a former clockmaker from Switzerland, could build almost any instrument or machine that he was asked to make.

The two others in the group were Sigmund Bergmann and Johann Schuckert. These talented electrical engineers left Edison & Unger years later to return to their native Germany. There, they founded two of the largest electrical manufacturing concerns in Western Europe.

These men, like Tom, were dedicated to their profession and were prepared to work hard and long. Tom's leadership was strong, and he directed his staff well. Though Tom was only twenty-four years old when he began, his word carried such authority that his group soon began calling him the "Old Man."

The nickname was only meant to poke gentle fun at Tom, for the men liked working at Edison & Unger. John Ott's first impression of Tom was that he was "as dirty as any of the other workmen, and not much better dressed than a tramp. But I immediately felt that there was a great deal to him."

Neither John Ott nor any of the others had ever worked for such a boss as Tom. He was young and friendly, full of humorous stories; yet he could quickly become very stern, forcing them to stick to their work and work even harder.

Tom's vast knowledge and endless curiosity fascinated his employees. If Tom suddenly had a new idea, he would tell the employees to stop working so that they could check out the new concept. If someone from outside came in with a new invention that he thought Tom could improve, Tom would have the workers drop what they were doing in order to work on the new "toy." Employees liked the idea that they never knew what each day might bring.

In short, working for Tom Edison was a challenge. Though he kept his staff working long hours, Tom could work even longer. His staff respected this and tried to be as dedicated to their own jobs as Tom was to his. Sometimes, when working on particularly difficult projects, Tom would openly challenge his craftsmen; he would make bets or offer prizes to the first one who could find the problem and make the machine work.

Another thing set Tom's business apart from an ordinary one. There was no bookkeeper to keep track of bills to be paid and money received. The only account he kept was the payroll. This was in keeping with his dislike of numbers and distrust of large amounts of money.

Tom had once tried having a bookkeeper, but that experience taught him only that bookkeepers were no use. The bookkeeper, at the end of the year, had found that there was a surplus of $7,500 cash. As the office was preparing to celebrate this extra money by throwing a big party, Tom went over the books himself. Then he remembered that he had not told the bookkeeper about several large payments. In the end, not only was there no surplus cash, but the company was actually several thousand dollars in debt.

From then on, Tom had his own system of "bookkeeping." On his desk he had one hook for bills and another hook for payments received. Rather than paying a bill when it was due, he would wait until a warning came in the mail that threatened to cut off service if he did not pay.

Paying bills was especially bothersome to Tom when he was working with his staff on a particularly interesting experiment or innovation. Because these extra projects paid little, if anything, Tom would have to direct his attention once again to producing his universal stock ticker in order to raise some cash. On such occasions, there was heavy pressure to raise money fast, for the warning that service would be cut off would be lying on Tom's desk. So Tom would put his staff on two shifts, day and night, until he could pay off the bill.

During Tom's first year in Newark he found another major distraction. She was a lovely, slightly plump, 15-year-old girl with golden hair. Her name was Mary Stilwell, and she worked in Tom's shop.

It is not clear just how Tom and Mary met. One account says that they met at the shop, after Mary had already been hired. Another account says that they met one rainy summer evening. Mary and her older sister, Alice, had been caught in the rain and were standing under the shop's doorway for shelter when Tom appeared on his way out.

Until that moment, Tom had had very little time or use for anything unrelated to work or science. But there was something about seeing those two girls beneath his doorstep that made him act differently this time. He greeted them politely and invited them to come up to his shop, out of the rain.

The two sisters, Tom learned, were Sunday school teachers who came from a poor, but respectable, family. Tom liked the two girls, but he especially liked the beautiful younger sister, Mary. When Tom returned to work the next day, he found himself still thinking of Mary and not thinking so much about his work. He was not used to being distracted this way!

Soon, Tom called on Mary and offered her a job at his shop punching holes into telegraph tape. Though Mary became part of a group doing this job, Tom watched only Mary. One laboratory assistant recalled that Mary was a quiet girl, far too shy to beg her boss not to stare at her while she worked. Instead, when Mary could not take Tom's stares any longer, she would simply drop her hands and telegraph tape into her lap. Then she would gaze up at Tom with a frustrated, helpless look on her face. Tom was enchanted.

Tom let neither his deafness nor his lack of experience with women stand in the way of gaining Mary's attention. In fact, Tom used his deafness to his advantage: it gave him an excuse for being close to Mary whenever she had to reply to something he had said. Still, Tom made no attempts at idle conversation, even with Mary. He was not used to chatting with anybody. Tom was probably all the more confused about how to talk with someone so shy and utterly charming.

For that reason, the two had rarely spoken to each other when one night he turned to her and, flashing a quick smile, asked, "What do you think of me, little girl, do you like me?"

Mary was stunned and flustered, but she was truthful: "Why, Mr. Edison, you frighten me. That is—I—"

"Don't be in a hurry about telling me," Tom replied. "It doesn't matter much, unless you would like to marry me."

Mary did not know whether to scream or laugh, but Tom was not disturbed. He told her to think it over and talk to her mother. Meanwhile, he eagerly awaited her reply.

CHAPTER TEN

The Quadruplex and the Robber Baron

Tom courted Mary with the same devotion and attention to detail that he showed in his work. Though he had rarely gone to church before, soon Tom and his business partner were often seen riding out in a horse-drawn carriage to Mary and Alice Stilwell's Sunday school. Tom also visited Mary at her home, under the watchful eye of her parents. It is said that Tom taught Mary the Morse code, tapping messages into the palm of her hand with a silver coin, so that they could speak together in private.

One day, Tom nervously approached Mr. Stilwell and asked for his daughter's hand in marriage.

"Mary is extremely young," Mr. Stilwell replied. "You'll have to wait at least a year."

"Sir, I don't think I can wait that long. I want to get married now," said Tom.

A few weeks later, on Christmas Day of 1871, Mr. Thomas Alva Edison and his new bride, Mary, emerged from a small family ceremony in Newark. After the wedding lunch, Tom brought Mary to their new home, a house he had bought a few days before.

Though Tom and Mary loved each other, it is also likely that both of them felt a little strange in their new roles. Tom recalled that just about an hour after the marriage ceremony, all he could think about were his stock tickers! "I told my wife about them and said I would like to go down to the factory," Tom said. "She agreed at once."

According to Tom, he returned home at dinnertime on his wedding day. However, others in the Edison family say that while Tom was at the factory, he got stuck on some technical problem and completely forgot about the time. It was only after his business partner discovered him still working at midnight that he remembered to go home. There, his young, frightened bride was tearfully waiting for him.

The next day, the newlyweds left for their honeymoon at Niagara Falls. But according to Edison history, Mary felt "so young and inexperienced" that she insisted her older sister, Alice, accompany them.

In fact, their marriage began as it was to continue throughout the years. Tom would become so involved with his work that sometimes he forgot to come home for days. Other times, he would come home so tired that all he could do was fall into bed. Alice Stilwell visited frequently to keep Mary company.

Mary Edison may not have understood the intricate details of Tom's work, but she knew it probably had to do with his telegraph machines. Mary knew how important the telegraph machines were to Tom—she had even worked on them herself. She also knew that Tom was forever short of cash, partly because of his bad bookkeeping. He was in a constant whirl trying to raise money, either by finding new investors or by making more stock tickers.

By 1872, Tom had improved his stock ticker and renamed it the Edison stock printer. One day, early in his marriage, Tom was given a rush order for thirty thousand dollars' worth of his stock printers. As usual, all hands concentrated on completing the order. Unfortunately, it turned out that the new model had a certain "bug" in it that kept it from working right. Tom was in a pinch, for his customer needed the printers right away and Tom did not want to lose the job—or the thirty thousand dollars.

With such an emergency upon him, Tom called together his core group of loyal assistants, including Charles Batchelor, John Kruesi, Sigmund Bergmann, and John Ott. He told them sternly that he was about to shut himself up with them in the top-floor laboratory until they had found what was causing the trouble.

"Now, you fellows," Tom said, "I've locked the door, and you'll have to stay here until this job is completed. Well," he sighed, "let's find the 'bugs.' "

For two and a half days straight, Tom and his group studied the machine, came up with possible solutions and experimented over and over. They had little food and less sleep. Some of the group's wives came knocking on the door and pleaded with Tom to let their husbands come home. But Tom was firm and would not open the door, even to let them drop off baskets of food. The men had no choice but to keep at their task until, at last, the machine worked perfectly.

That same year, Tom took out thirty-eight new patents for new models or new parts of his stock machine. There were telegraph type-wheels, several printing devices, and relay magnets. Patent laws, both then and now, apply to even little improvements on existing machines. This encourages scientists to make more technological advances and to receive the proper credit for them.

In the scientific world, Tom Edison was developing a fine reputation as a young wonder who could improve the kinks in almost any machine. One day, that reputation led a man named Edward H. Johnson to Tom's Newark factory door. Mr. Johnson brought with him a model of what he called an automatic telegraph machine, invented by a certain George D. Little.

Little's automatic telegraph used a moving paper tape with holes punched into it. Those holes matched the Morse code dots and dashes. At the receiving end, the dots and dashes were printed out on paper. This was supposed to make it easier and quicker for the telegraphers to copy the message. The trouble, Mr. Johnson said, was that over a distance of more than two hundred miles, Little's machine was slow. It was even slower than the old machines, and the print was often hard to read.

Mr. Johnson said he represented a group of investors who had thought the machine would prove to be a commercial success. The group had even formed a company named the Automatic Telegraph Company, and they were looking for more investors. But because the machine didn't work too well, no one wanted to join them. Mr. Johnson said he had heard that Tom might be able to fix the machine. Tom said he would look it over.

Tom was intrigued by the new telegraph machine. A few days later, he told Mr Johnson that he thought he could improve it. Right away, the Automatic Telegraph Company had Tom sign a contract that said the improvements he made on the machine would belong to them. In return, Tom would be able to use their money to carry out his experiments.

With that, Tom was given forty thousand dollars to start work on the project. With a friend, Joseph Murray, as his partner, Tom opened up a second shop in Newark called Edison & Murray. They bought special equipment and material, hired a staff and set to work on the automatic telegraph.

Tom never tired of trying to improve the telegraph, for he knew how important the machine was. By that time, the telegraph and Morse code had been around nearly twenty-five years, and more and more people had come to depend on it. In many ways, the telegraph served the same purpose as the telephone does today. It was a link between people who lived far apart from each other. It quickly transmitted word of disaster or emergency. And of course, it helped trade and commerce.

Whenever Tom was called upon to improve a device, he felt it was necessary to know everything about it up to that point. So when he began to tackle the automatic telegraph, he quickly set to studying. Mr. Johnson recalled Tom's work habits:

> I came in one night and there sat Edison with a pile of chemical books that were five feet high when laid one upon another. He had ordered them from New York, London and Paris. He studied them night and day. He ate at his desk and slept in a chair. In six weeks he had gone through the books, written a volume of abstracts (in which he told briefly in his own words what a book said), made two thousand experiments . . . and produced a solution, the only one that could do the thing he wanted.

By early 1872, Tom was ready to test out his automatic telegraph lines. Over the next few months, he experimented until the automatic telegraph could transmit one thousand words a minute in Morse code signals. (Compare that to early telegraphers' top speed of forty-five words a minute!) In addition to speeding up the process, Tom improved the paper tape at the receiving end, as well as the punching machine that made the holes in the tape.

Despite these new improvements and the patents he received on them, Tom was not satisfied. In the midst of all the experiments, another idea had occurred to him. If the automatic telegraph could print out dots and dashes at the receiving end, why couldn't it print out regular roman letters instead? Tom and his assistants worked on answering that question for the next four months.

In the end, the automatic telegraph that printed letters was much slower than the Morse code printer. The new, roman-letter printing machine transmitted only two hundred and fifty words a minute, against the Morse's one thousand. Still, this was six times faster than the original way of doing it by hand.

By the summer of 1872, Tom wanted to put an end to manufacturing stock printers. He was eager to get to work again on the telegraph. He knew this meant no more income from Western Union, but Tom did not care. He did not like his business partner either, and was only too happy to pay Unger what was due to be rid of him.

The more Tom worked on his much-loved telegraph, the more excited the Automatic Telegraph Company became. The telegraph was clearly becoming a better and ever more important instrument.

Unfortunately, the control of the telegraph industry was falling into greedy hands. The main person behind this was an American financier named Jay Gould. Since the 1860s, Gould had been buying up the railroad lines—illegally—and making millions of dollars. But Gould also wanted to control the telegraph and newspaper industries, as well as the railroad. This would make him not only wealthier but very powerful too. Meanwhile, the American people would suffer.

From the late 1860s through the 1870s, Gould worked out his scheme. As owner of the railroad and telegraph services, the wily businessman would control all the train and telegraph routes, ticket prices and service.

By controlling the news industry, Gould would control which stories could or could not be reported.

This short, dark, black-bearded man was much more clever, and had much higher goals, than an ordinary thief. Gould did not choose to rob houses or stores. His targets were the stock and gold markets. In the fall of 1869, he had managed to cheat the gold market so successfully that he caused the United States to go into a temporary depression. By owning the railroads, as well as the newspaper and telegraph wire services, Gould figured he could control everything that influenced the stock and gold markets. With the markets under his control, he could make unlimited amounts of money! By 1873, Gould was already known as "the destroying angel of Wall Street."

When Tom revealed his inventions and improvements on the automatic telegraph, the true head of the Automatic Telegraph Company finally revealed himself—and it was none other than Jay Gould. With Tom's inventions and patents, Gould planned to set up a telegraph service that would compete with Western Union's telegraph empire. Ultimately, Gould wanted to buy out Western Union (just as Western Union had bought out Tom's stock ticker service a few years earlier). The only difference was that Gould would be willing to cheat to do so.

To Tom, however, it mattered little that Gould was the head of the company. Tom was too involved with perfecting the machine to pay much attention to politics and outside matters. All that mattered to him was having the money to continue his experiments, and Jay Gould allowed him to do that. Gould had also given Tom and his partner orders to manufacture their new automatic telegraph.

By then, Tom was a father to a baby daughter named Marion, whom he nicknamed "Dot," after the Morse code. When his son, Thomas, Jr. was born in 1876, Tom nicknamed him "Dash." (His youngest son, born in 1878, was named William Leslie and had no nickname.)

The telegraph was truly the most important thing in Tom's life. Tom felt he was on the verge of making his biggest telegraph dream come true. He wanted to make a "quadruplex." This new telegraph machine would send four messages, two going out and two coming in at the same time. He had been trying to put together such a machine since his early telegraph days. To work on his dream machine, Tom got financial support from Western Union, as well as permission to experiment on their wires after hours.

Tom's first step was to make his own duplex machine, like the one J. B. Stearns had invented, only better. After much work, Tom created his own duplex, which was able to send one message out and take one message in at the same time. Tom's next invention was the "diplex," which could send two messages out at the same time. Tom considered this a great leap toward creating his dream machine: basically, all he had to do was somehow combine the two machines to make the quadruplex.

At that point, however, Tom needed more money to continue his research. With these two recent and remarkable achievements to his credit, Tom was sure Western Union would be glad to continue working with him. Oddly enough, Western Union ignored Tom. The company did not seem the slightest bit interested in what he had done, even though his inventions could more than double Western Union's business.

To work on his quadruplex, Tom desperately needed money. He turned to his other money source, Jay Gould's Automatic Telegraph Company. By then, Gould's small telegraph service had already begun to cut into Western Union's business. Tom's inventions pleased Gould, and he lent Tom money for further development.

For the next year, Tom and his team buried themselves in thought, process and experiments and finally produced a successful invention. But Edison was also forced to bounce between both companies for money. Neither company would give Tom more than a fraction of his costs, and Tom was badly in debt. Both companies were taking advantage of Tom and his dedicated group, and Edison knew it. Still, making the quadruplex was more important. He was willing to sacrifice almost anything, even his pride, to complete his machine.

The quadruplex, completed in the summer of 1874, was then considered Tom Edison's crowning achievement. Though this machine no longer exists, it was a fantastic combination of sounders, circuits, condensers, batteries and relays that only a truly scientific and ingenious mind could construct. Not only did the machine work, it did so accurately, harmoniously and without fail. Scientists around the world marveled at his invention, which applied electricity in a revolutionary manner.

The importance of the quadruplex was clear to both Western Union and the Automatic Telegraph Company. Whichever company owned the quadruplex would dominate the industry. Since Tom had been forced to work for both companies to invent the machine, it was not clear who owned the rights to it. The two companies were in court over the matter for the next seven years. In the end, Gould got his original wish: he took control of Western Union.

Tom, meanwhile, was never paid by either company for the quadruplex. But Tom had no regrets, for he had invented his dream. It was now time to turn to other inventions.

CHAPTER ELEVEN

The Independent Inventor

ZZZP! CRACK! SMASH!

"What in tarnation—!"

"But, Mr. Edison, all I did was take this wire and charge it to that and—"

"Hmmm . . . Now, I wonder why that happened. Tell me again what you did . . ."

The top floor of Tom Edison's factory in Newark may have sounded something like that during the hectic days. The year after the quadruplex invention, Edison explored new areas of science that he thought might lead to more useful inventions This course led to many different types of experiments—and lots of unexpected results.

Edison was fairly understanding when his own or his assistants' experiments came out wrong or exploded, for he was always curious about *why* something had occurred. Though all the workers in the Edison laboratory were highly skilled and dedicated, they were all still learning. That included Edison.

In the magazines and reports Edison read, scientists

and inventors in the United States and Europe were coming up with many new ideas and devices to make life easier. For example, a few years before, a man named Christopher Sholes had come up with something called a typewriter.

The first model of his typewriter was a roughly made device, so Sholes took it to Edison for improvement. With Edison's help, an improved typewriter was produced. The machine brought major changes to the business world. Records could be kept more exactly. Letters could be written faster. For the first time, it was common to see large numbers of women in offices, for they were hired to do the typing.

Another man, Cyrus Field, had come up with telegraph cable so strong that it could be laid at the bottom of the ocean. It could stretch from the United States to Great Britain without breaking! This meant that news could travel quickly between the United States, England and the rest of Europe. Bankers and businesspeople were especially happy to be able to keep close contact with their colleagues abroad.

By 1875 the words *growth* and *progress* were on nearly every American's lips. The United States had entered into a busy, booming period that was changing everyday life.

Back in 1850, when Edison was a toddler watching wagon trains head West, the United States had a smaller population than Great Britain. But in the next twenty-five years, the population had boomed from twenty-three million to forty million, and the nation was still growing.

The steel, coal and oil industries were also beginning

to thrive. Steel was used to construct large bridges, buildings, trains, and factories. Coal was burned to produce power for factories and railroads. Oil from beneath the earth's surface, first drilled for only sixteen years earlier, was now being used to keep machines running smoothly and to light lamps.

Trains made it easier and faster to travel. The telegraph and now the quadruplex were making communication easier, and faster too. In the previous few years, mail service had grown and improved as well. In 1863, mail carriers delivered only in cities, but now mail was delivered in smaller towns too. And as towns and cities grew across the nation, there were places to go and lots of people to send and receive messages.

The Civil War had brought freedom for slaves. Along with that freedom, a new law (taken back in 1883) let black people use the same trains, trolley cars, hotels and other public facilities as white people.

To most Americans, the world was suddenly becoming amazingly advanced and modern. They could not imagine what new invention, industry or law would change their world next.

One invention that caught Edison's eye that year was something called an electric arc light. This light, he had read, was brightening the streets of Russia, Germany and France. The lights were hooked up to an electric dynamo, a machine that produced currents of electricity. The arc was really a giant spark that jumped from one carbon rod to another nearby rod. The current that flowed across the gap superheated the air in between and created light. Arc lights were good for street lighting, but they were too big and bright for indoors, where candles and whale oil or kerosene gas lamps were used.

Still, Edison tried making his own arc light in his laboratory. He connected two exposed carbon points with an extra-large battery. The light did not last more than a minute or two. He pursued this experiment a while longer, but soon he turned his attention to something else.

Another project that interested Edison was something he called acoustical telegraphy. That meant basic telegraphy—but with sound vibrations sent over the wire. Edison thought that by varying the sound patterns, he might find new ways of sending more messages over the wire at once. In fact, acoustical telegraphy was one of the last stages before the telephone was invented.

Edison worked on acoustical telegraphy for some months and made several new discoveries about electricity in the process. But after receiving patents on those discoveries, he soon laid those experiments aside, too.

Edison's business was doing well. He had the respect of scientists and investors alike, but felt it was time for a big change in his life. He no longer wanted to be in the manufacturing business, forced to confine his inventing to the sidelines. He wanted to invent full-time, on his own, away from the bustle of Newark. Edison knew exactly what he wanted, and one day he acted on that wish.

In the spring of 1876, Edison moved his laboratory, his core of assistants, wife and two children to the tiny village of Menlo Park in the New Jersey countryside. The Edisons lived in a plain farmhouse near his newly built laboratory. Two of the village's six houses became homes for the families of Charles Batchelor and John Kruesi; the other assistants, single men, lived in the village boarding houses. Before long, Menlo Park had changed from a sleepy village to one mostly devoted to Tom Edison's scientific experiments and inventions. Some of the villagers took to calling their town "Edison Village," and it was no wonder.

Soon after Edison was settled in Menlo Park, Western Union asked him to resume his work on acoustical telegraphy. This was particularly hard for Edison, because of his bad hearing. But by biting into sound instruments, he could sense the sound vibrations traveling from his head to his inner hearing nerve.

At the same time, a young Scotsman who had moved to the United States was working on something he called the telephone. The man, Alexander Graham Bell, had been working on the device for some time. That summer, he finally heard the first weak sounds of his assistant's voice coming over his crude wire. By winter, Mr. Bell received a patent on his invention.

To Mr. Bell's surprise, Western Union's president, William Orton, was not at all interested in his telephone.

"What can we do with such an electrical toy?" Mr. Orton asked the Scotsman.

"Why, telephones could one day replace the telegraph system, sir," replied Mr. Bell.

Mr. Orton just shook his head. To him, Alexander Bell was just another inventor with wild ideas. Mr. Bell's

Tom and Mary Stilwell Edison and their house in Menlo Park, New Jersey.

invention was interesting, he thought, but hardly practical.

This original telephone was extremely simple. Instead of having a receiver for listening and a mouthpiece for speaking, a single instrument did both. This made it difficult to hear and talk back at the same time. Also, people could speak to each other from only two miles away at the most. Even then, they had to shout each sentence three or four times to be heard.

However, when Mr. Bell demonstrated his telephone at the Centennial Exposition in Philadelphia a year later, it caused a public sensation. After that, Western Union was interested. But by then, Mr. Bell had already formed his own company, Bell Telephone. Now Western Union was a little worried.

So Western Union did the next best thing: it went to Tom Edison. The company wanted him to improve Mr. Bell's telephone. It wanted Edison's improvements to be so great that people would want Western Union's Edison telephone, not the Bell telephone.

Six months later, Edison had come up with a number of improvements that made his telephone better than Mr. Bell's. But Edison was still not satisfied. He needed a stronger transmitter that would made the message clearer over long distances. This was the hardest part of all, because he did not know what substance would make the best transmitter.

For Edison, the only way to find the right substance was to try and try, and then try some more. To begin, Edison and his staff tried every chemical in the laboratory—some two thousand of them! Even after all that, not one chemical was the right one. These experiments were especially hard for Edison, because he could not hear for himself how a certain chemical sounded on the transmitter. His assistants were Edison's ears, and from their information, Edison had to guess what else might work.

The key substance, it turned out, was carbon. The first carbon Edison used was taken from a piece of burned, broken glass. He scraped off the smoky, black carbon and molded it into a small ball. It was only the size of a button. After a few more adjustments, Edison tried it and—success! Near-deaf as he was, even Edison could hear on his telephone! His own handicap had helped him make sure of the telephone's most important advances.

Eventually, Bell Telephone bought the rights to Edison's improvements from Western Union. Western Union paid Tom $100,000 for his carbon transmitter, and Bell Telephone became the nation's major phone system for the next hundred years.

Making the telephone carbon transmitter did not make Tom Edison famous, but his next major invention did. This particular invention grew out of his experiments in improving the telephone.

Tinkering with sound and sound instruments had fascinated Tom Edison and given him new ideas. When Edison finished with the telephone transmitter, he started working on an idea that had occurred to him while working on the telephone. He thought he could make a machine that would repeat the sound of a voice.

Edison, his improved telephone, and workers testing a phono-
graphic record.

After many months, his idea became a real working model. He built it, experimented on it and improved it. Edison called his device a phonograph, from the Greek words for *sound* and *write*. He experimented privately on his machine, trying to find the best way to get sound from it. Finally, Edison came up with what he thought would make a good first model. Since he was not as handy at building as his assistants were, he sketched his model on paper and gave the sketch to John Kruesi.

Kruesi built the model exactly as Edison had sketched it. The machine was made of brass and iron. It had a slender cylinder set on a long shaft, with a hand crank to turn it.

Though it looked strange, Edison was fairly confident it would work. First, a thin, metal disc would receive sound waves, just as in Bell's telephone. A tiny pin at the center of the disc would scratch an impression of a sheet of tinfoil wrapped around the cylinder. As the crank turned, the pin would move to the right and the cylinder would revolve.

As the cylinder went around, the pin would make a spiral groove on the tinfoil. This groove would make a pattern that matched the voice. Edison then attached a second pin to a second disc. This picked up the voice pattern and turned it into vibrations, which would produce the sound.

But Tom Edison did not explain the phonograph to anyone.

When Kruesi was nearly finished making Edison's model, he asked, "What is this machine for, anyway?"

"Well," said Edison, "if all goes right, it might just repeat my voice when I speak into it."

"But that's absurd!" Kruesi exclaimed.

Though Edison thought his idea was good, secretly he did not expect it to work. Still, it might give him something to work on in the future. Kruesi called the other assistants around as Edison sat down with his new machine.

Slowly, Edison started turning the hand crank, while he shouted onto the little discs, "Mary had a little lamb, its fleece was white as snow . . ."

His assistants looked at each other, as if to say, "Our boss is crazy!"

When Edison finished reciting the nursery rhyme, he turned the crank back to the starting point and made the proper adjustments. He then turned the crank forward again and suddenly, from out of the machine, came Edison's very own voice reciting, "Mary had a little lamb, its fleece was white as snow!"

"Good heavens!" shouted Kruesi.

Edison and his other assistants were equally astonished. He did the experiment for them again and again. Then they all stayed up for the rest of the night. They fixed and adjusted the new phonograph until they got better and better results. They tried the machine over and over, listening to their voices coming back to them. Each time they did, they were truly amazed.

The American public reacted much the same way. They could not understand how such a simple-looking machine could replay the sound of their own voices! It was magic, they thought, or a trick! Some thought there was a hidden person in the room, repeating what they said. But when the machine could repeat even the strangest message, those who had doubted were satisfied that the machine really worked.

Tom Edison had invented the first record player. At the time, Edison thought his machine would be used mostly for business. It would be handy for dictating letters and recording personal notes. He thought some people would use it for playing music, but he had no idea how popular it would become for that. Since Edison was so hard of hearing, he never listened to music or had much use for it. Also, his first machine did not produce a good sound at all, and music came out sounding funny. But the American people did not care. Edison's machine delighted and thrilled them!

Suddenly, Menlo Park became a major tourist attraction for Americans and foreigners alike. Edison invited the public to come right inside his laboratory. He wanted the world to see everything possible. And see they did! People were astounded at all the chemical jars, metals, batteries, electric machines and crazy-looking inventions that filled his workroom. Tangled telephone and telegraph wires hung from the ceiling like vines in a jungle.

When the visitors were finished looking, Edison would answer questions. Most people would ask him about the phonograph, and he would happily demonstrate the machine and explain how it worked. People

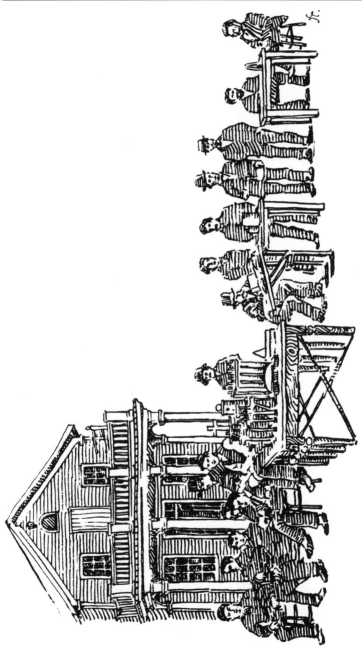

The Edison staff in front of the Menlo Park laboratory.

liked listening to Tom Edison. He was a young, friendly man who could explain things in plain language.

Soon, Edison was even called to the White House. There, he gave a demonstration of his amazing "talking machine" to President Rutherford B. Hayes. To Americans, Tom Edison was a national hero. Some people called him a genius, to which Edison replied, "Genius is ninety-nine percent perspiration and one percent inspiration." In other words, Edison felt that with a lot of hard, hard work and a little imagination, anyone could be a genius.

But people just shook their heads at that. Tom Edison could do *anything*! He was the "Wizard of Menlo Park!"

CHAPTER TWELVE

The Search for the Electric Light

O ne morning, in the spring of 1878, Edison woke up and stared at the ceiling. He did not feel like moving or eating or going to the lab. He did not feel like doing *anything*, anything at all.

The Wizard of Menlo Park was, simply, tired! After years and years of working nonstop, night and day, experimenting and inventing, failing and succeeding, Tom Edison needed a long rest away from his lab.

A friend of Edison's, a college professor named George Barker, invited him on a trip out West. Edison eagerly accepted the invitation. A change of scenery was just the cure for him.

The two first went to the Colorado Rocky Mountains, where they and some other scientists watched an eclipse of the sun. Then Edison and Professor Barker rode the train from Nebraska to California, only Edison did not ride in the usual passenger seat. Instead, the engineers let him ride the whole way outside on the train's cowcatcher (the metal grating on the outside of the train). To Tom Edison, this was a glorious adventure!

During the two months that Edison was away, Professor Barker spoke to him about doing some new experiments when he returned. He wanted Edison to find a way to put electric lighting inside homes. Edison liked the idea. He was ready to start on something new, and this particular idea would be a great challenge.

Though arc lights were already brightening the streets of some cities in Europe and now in the United States too, lighting for homes had not changed in six thousand years! Oil lamps were still the best kind of artificial light. But the oil smelled, it was expensive, and it was only brighter than a candle, not bright enough to light a room a night. Candles were cheap and didn't smell, but they could not light a house well either.

For many years, people had wanted better lights for their homes. Scientists had tried to come up with ways to make them, but without success. They had begun experimenting in 1801 and had continued on and off since then. But with electric arc lights springing up, scientists once again tried to make a good light for home use. This time, they felt closer to the answer than ever before. Every scientist wanted to be the first to discover how to adapt the electric arc light for use in the home. Unofficially, the race was on.

When Edison returned from his trip, he was fully refreshed and ready to start on his new project. He only worried that he was starting too late. He thought other scientists might have already beaten him to the solution.

Soon, Edison went to visit a man named William Wallace, who had built a series of eight glaring arc lights.

Each contained five hundred candlepower (or the amount of light that five hundred candles would give). All the lights were connected to an electric dynamo that generated the power. The dynamo was eight horsepower, or as strong as eight horses.

Seeing Mr. Wallace's setup, Edison smiled to himself. He studied the lights and then the dynamo; then looked at the lights again. He sat down at a table and began calculating, still chuckling to himself.

What Edison realized was that this kind of light setup was not at all what was needed in the home. Running it would take hundreds of pounds of coal, which most people could neither afford nor store.

Arc lamps use a lot of current. To make them practical, they were connected in what is called a series circuit. This means that the current flows out of the dynamo into the first lamp. When it flows out of the first lamp, the same current then goes into the second lamp, and so on. In this way, the same current could light many lamps. However, if one lamp goes out, the circuit is interrupted, and all the lamps go out. If you lighted your house by this system, you could not turn off one lamp and leave all the others on.

Edison wanted to develop a system in which some lights could be on and some could be off within a home. He wanted that to be true from house to house too. The electric light system he would develop would have to take an entirely different approach from the theory behind the arc light.

Turning to Mr. Wallace, Edison said, "I believe I can

beat you in making the electric light. I do not think you are working in the right direction."

Mr. Wallace thought to himself, If Mr. Edison thinks he can beat me, well, that's fine. I'll just have to prove him wrong. Aloud, he said, "Okay, Mr. Edison, prove it!"

They both laughed and shook hands.

After leaving Mr. Wallace's place, Edison thought more about what he had seen and felt relieved. As he later recalled, "I saw the thing had not gone so far but that I had a chance."

What Mr. Wallace and other scientists like him were not doing, Edison thought, was finding a way to subdivide light. That is, Edison wanted to break the system down into many smaller lights, so that it could be brought into private houses.

Edison's first great idea for electric lighting was the parallel circuit. The idea was to feed electricity to lamps the way gas was fed. The main gas pipe feeds into a lot of smaller pipes. Every fixture was on its own branch, so each gaslight could be turned on or off without affecting the others. Edison's parallel circuit divided the current from the dynamo in this way. Each lamp would use only a small part of the current. The next problem was to invent an electric light that would work on a small current.

Looking to the future, Tom Edison saw a central station for electric lighting. From that station, a network of electric wires would extend as far as necessary to deliver electric current to a home. Somehow, Edison thought, the amount of current could also be measured, or metered, and sold. That way, people would pay for only the amount of electricity their home used.

Feeling perhaps overly confident, Edison told a reporter how he saw the future electric home light. Tom Edison's theory would prove to be absolutely right. But his declaration that he would have the electric light ready *in six weeks* was wrong.

There was much, much work to be done. First, Edison wanted to come up with a light that used very little current. Turning to his research books, he found out that scientists had made the first "glow lamps" as far back as 1820. In those lamps, little metallic or carbon burners had been placed in tightly sealed glass tubes. Those were the first incandescent lamps, the kind that Edison knew would fulfill a home's needs. The trouble with the early lamps was that they did not burn for more than a few minutes. Edison needed to find out why and to discover a way to correct the problem.

The basic difficulty was the light's filament, the thread-like wire that causes a lamp to burn. The filament has to be very thin in order to heat up from the small currents produced by high voltages. The trouble with filaments, as Edison soon found out, was that because they have to be so thin, they break easily. Filaments also burn out quickly when in contact with oxygen in the air, and they melt from the high temperatures involved.

Edison would tackle these problems. But his first step was to find the right substance with which to make his filament. He needed a material that had a high melting

Edison examines a series of experimental light bulbs.

point—that is, a metal that would not melt when it glowed at a high temperature.

The first substance he tried was carbon, the material he used with his successful telephone transmitter. Unfortunately, his experiments with the carbon filament were not successful. Within eight minutes the lamp had burned out.

Next, he experimented with a whole range of metals and settled on platinum. Though carbon had a higher melting point than platinum, Edison was able to bring the platinum wire to a brilliant light inside the glass bulb. This light did not last long either, but Edison was able to find ways to control the heat inside the bulb. If the wire did not get too hot, it would last a few minutes longer. Even so, his devices were not always reliable, which exasperated Edison a great deal. Still, he felt that he was at least on the right track.

Next, he began to search for a way to keep oxygen from seeping into the glass bulbs. In those days, the pumps that vacuumed air out of glass tubes had not been perfected yet, and air leakage was common. This was another reason why filaments burned out quickly. At the same time, Edison was working out his plan of using parallel circuits to send electricity into homes. The one thing he knew for sure was that all these experiments would take a lot of money to work out.

A lawyer for Western Union named Grosvenor Lowrey became the strongest link between the inventor and his investors. Mr. Lowrey, who liked Edison and had great faith in his abilities, began seeking out his own wealthiest clients in New York. He asked them to support Tom Edison's research for the incandescent light.

After Edison's success with the platinum wire, he called in two New York reporters. To newspapers, anything done or said by "the man who invented the phonograph" was considered a news story.

Edison told the reporters that he had already figured out how to turn electricity into a cheap and practical substitute for gaslights. This went way beyond Edison's progress at that point, but nobody knew that.

That interview was just the first of a series of interviews Tom Edison gave, in which he exaggerated how close he really was to the solution. Edison did this with Grosvenor Lowrey's encouragement. Mr. Lowrey felt that public enthusiasm and publicity would help his potential investors see the wisdom of helping Edison.

In another interview, Edison predicted that there would soon be a day when it would be possible to transmit energy for light, as well as for heating, cooking and running an elevator or a sewing machine. Shortly after these "wild" predictions, Edison was forced to admit that he was still looking for the perfect substance with which to light his glass bulb.

Nevertheless, at the end of six weeks, Edison told a reporter that he had, indeed, made the perfect light.

"Is it an electric light?" asked the reporter.

"An electric light and nothing else," Tom Edison boasted. He explained that the light was connected to a new type of dynamo.

"We simply turn the power of steam into electricity," he said. "The greater the steam power we obtain, the more electricity we get." Of course, Edison was careful to add that he needed time, perhaps a few months or even a year, to "get the bugs out," and perfect his light and light system.

But to prove to the reporter that his electric light worked, Tom Edison turned on his platinum-wire glass bulb. The reporter gave this account: "The new light came on, cold and beautiful. . . . The strip of platinum that acted as a burner *did not burn*. It was incandescent."

115

The reporter said the bulb glowed like a star until, with a simple turn of a screw, the brightness went out.

What the reporter did not know at the time, and what Edison purposely did not tell him, was that the light would have gone off by itself a few minutes later. Though his model looked good it was still far from perfect.

On the same occasion, Edison boasted that he would soon light up all of downtown New York City with half a million incandescent lamps, which would be powered by just a few steam dynamos. This statement caused great excitement in both the United States and Europe.

There was such expectation for electricity that stocks and securities in gaslight declined dramatically. The only people to voice their predictions of doom and failure were, naturally, the scientists competing with Tom Edison, and men in the gas industry.

The large and exaggerated stories in the newspapers soon brought Edison what he and Mr. Lowrey wanted: financial support. Western Union, along with Mr. Lowrey's wealthy group of clients, agreed to buy the rights to Tom Edison's electric light and distributing system. This group of capitalists, which included the rich and powerful Morgan and Vanderbilt families, gave Edison 1301fifty thousand dollars to begin his research. This established the Edison Electric Light Company.

Edison's investors were willing to support his new, not-yet-created invention. Why? Because Tom Edison had such a record of achievement, the investors felt sure their money was in the right hands.

Now the grind began for real. Though the newspaper stories had won Edison the necessary money, they had also brought him increased pressure. The eyes of the world were on him now. All waited and watched for his predictions to come true. Tom Edison also had a group of powerful, anxious and impatient investors to please—yet he still had not even found the right substance for his light!

CHAPTER THIRTEEN

The Needle in the Haystack

Edison set to work with a happy gleam in his eye. He was bursting with energy, purpose and new ideas. Each time his experimental lamp failed to stay lit, Edison would be ready with another idea to try.

"I never allow myself to become discouraged, under any circumstances," Tom Edison once wrote. Even if he had tried five hundred or a thousand different variations on an experiment and not one had worked, Tom would not lose confidence. Rather, he would feel that he had learned five hundred or a thousand ways *not* to proceed with the experiment.

"We sometimes learn a lot from our failures, if we have put into the effort the best thought and work we are capable of," Edison wrote.

With this attitude, Edison took up his search for the perfect light and lighting system. Most people would have found such an optimistic outlook hard to keep up, especially under such pressure. In fact, trouble started almost as soon as the news was out about Tom Edison's newest, and now financially secure, project.

Now that Edison had his investors, there was no longer a need to publicize his experiments and progress. If anything, he wanted total secrecy. But, somehow, rumors leaked out and found their way to the press. First came the newspaper stories. They reported that the Wizard of Menlo Park was "ill" or "worn out" by all his experimenting. The stories also added that his experiments had not led anywhere, except to great disappointments.

Edison's friend and supporter, Mr. Lowrey, quickly denied the reports. "Mr. Edison is in good health and spirits," he declared. He added that Mr. Edison was "on the threshold of a new and wonderful development of electrical science."

On top of that, other scientists in the United States and Europe suddenly started claiming that they had "beaten" Edison in making the first indoor lamp. These claims later proved to be false. Still, the mere suggestion that others might win the electric light race made Edison's investors nervous. The rumors, combined with the reports in the newspapers about Edison's poor health and failing experiments, caused the investors to panic. They went so far as to suggest that Edison join up with two of the scientists who had made claims against him.

That made Edison angry. "It's the same old story!" he exclaimed. "No confidence in me. No one trusted that I could fix the telephone or invent the phonograph or do many other things!

"I refuse to join up with anyone," he said firmly.

119

"Naturally, other scientists will make claims! Anyone working in the same direction as I am would do that.

"But I have no fear of the result," Edison said. "What I am developing is entirely original and out of the rut."

After that, Tom Edison's investors sat back for a while and let him work.

Tom Edison knew that if his lamp was to light with small current, it had to work at high voltage. He planned to use about 120 volts instead of the 10 or 12 volts that was then in use. To glow with small current, the filament had to be extremely thin. He set out to find a material that could carry the current, could be made into a thin, strong wire and would not melt when it got hot. It also had to be readily available so that his lamps would not be too expensive.

Edison continued to experiment with the platinum wire, which he had set in a spiral inside the glass bulb. The bulb had had as much air taken out of it as possible with the laboratory's hand pump. The results were encouraging: the lamp would burn for an hour or two.

Edison tried many other materials, including carbon once again because it had the highest melting point. He thought of tungsten, which is used in bulbs today, but at that time he had no tools delicate enough to handle it. However, no metal seemed to last as long as platinum, even though platinum still did not last long enough.

For a while, Edison gave up his search for the perfect substance and instead searched for a better air pump. He went through all his scientific magazines and discovered that a new, improved pump was made in England. Called the Sprengel pump, it trapped air bubbles and sent them outside. Edison immediately ordered one. In the meantime, he found out that he could borrow one from nearby Princeton University.

Finally, Edison's assistant arrived with Princeton's Sprengel pump. Tom was so eager to try it out that he kept his assistants pumping until dawn. The results were good. The vacuum in the bulb now came very close to being completely airtight. The platinum wire shone at a brilliant twenty-five candlepower, instead of its usual four candlepower. Edison realized that in taking more air out, he had also taken out certain gases that had been preventing the platinum from burning so brightly.

That discovery was important enough for Edison to patent. It was the first recorded high-resistance platinum lamp with an improved vacuum.

Tom Edison felt good about his discovery. He also felt he had to do something to give heart to his financial supporters. So he did what he had done earlier—he reported the story to the newspapers.

"I've got a nearly perfect vacuum!" he declared. He also said that platinum was the perfect metal. All he needed was more platinum to make more lamps. To find it, Edison reported, he would be sending mining prospectors to the Rocky Mountains.

That was the last thing his investors wanted to hear. Platinum was then, and still is, a rare metal; therefore, it is very expensive. On top of that, Edison was rapidly running through his research money. To his investors, it did not appear that Edison was at all near the solution; yet he already needed more money.

In addition, it bothered the financial group to see big streetlights going up all over lower New York City although so little light seemed to be coming from Menlo Park. They were not at all sure Edison was on the right track.

To soothe their doubts, Mr. Lowrey once again stepped in. He arranged for some of the investors to tour Tom Edison's laboratory and get a private demonstration of the electric lamp thus far. That way, they could see exactly what was happening with their money. Edison did not like the idea, but he eventually gave in.

The visit did not go well.

The men came to Menlo Park late one afternoon in April 1879. Edison showed them around, explaining how his lab was set up and discussing various projects on which his staff members were working. He then showed them the platinum coils he was using in his lamps and explained the type of energy-producing dynamo he was making. By that time, the laboratory had grown dark. It was time for a demonstration of his light bulb.

"All right, Kruesi," Edison said, indicating it was time to turn on the dynamo, "turn on the juice slowly."

Slowly, the lamps started to glow to a cherry-red color.

"A little more juice," Edison instructed.

The lamps glowed brightly, with one shining like a star. Suddenly, PUFF! All the lamps went out, and the room fell into total darkness. Charles Batchelor quickly replaced the bad bulb in the series, but the next one went out as well. After two more tries, the demonstration ended.

Edison and his group went to the library for a discussion.

"The platinum coils seem to consume a lot of energy for the light they give," commented one investor.

"Platinum seems neither economical nor the best substance," said another.

Tom Edison tried to defend his system. "It's not the platinum," he said. "It's the dynamo, which is only a temporary one and heats up badly. Besides," Edison continued, "I could show you only a working model. I'm building one with a much better vacuum than the one you saw."

The investors were not convinced. One man said he had been reading of the vacuum experiments done in 1845 by a scientist named Starr. "It seems to me it would have been better to spend a few dollars for a copy of [Mr. Starr's book] and to begin where he left off," the man said, "rather than spend fifty thousand dollars to come independently to the same stopping point."

For a moment, Edison was speechless. This businessman was saying that Edison had discovered nothing new, nothing more than what another man had found out thirty-four years before. Edison then tried to explain that his light, the incandescent light, could not be found where Starr had left off.

Starr had passed over the answer, Edison said, adding, "So have I. That is why I want to go back over it again."

The businessmen just shook their heads. They were not scientists and just did not understand.

After that gloomy meeting, new rumors came out in the newspapers. They told of the disappointing platinum lamps. Gaslight securities went up and stock in the Edison Electric Light Company went down.

"What Has Mr. Edison Discovered?" asked the title of an article in a leading newspaper. In the article, several electricians said they doubted Tom Edison was on the right track. It also quoted a rival inventor, who said that Edison's newest patent showed "nothing new" and that his efforts were doomed to be miserable failures.

Edison paid no attention to the newspapers and rumors. The meeting, however, had forced him to rethink what he had learned.

Edison did know how to make an improved vacuum and how to raise the heat resistance of his metal coil. But he also realized that, despite all of the time he had put into developing it, platinum was not the answer. If anything, platinum was an obstacle. So it was back to the drawing board—and now Tom Edison had to move fast.

There were several things that Edison had to try at once. He did this by dividing his staff into groups. Each one carried out his instructions. One group reworked his electric current distribution system. Another checked the design and circuitry of his dynamo. A third group tried to perfect the pumping methods in taking air from the

Edison confers with an assistant in the laboratory.

lamp bulbs. Finally, his own group tested different materials to burn inside the lamp.

Edison's way of going about finding the right substance drove one of his assistants, Nikola Tesla, nearly crazy. Tesla once declared that if Edison had to find a needle in a haystack, he would diligently examine straw after straw of hay until he found the needle.

Tesla thought Edison should make more calculated experiments. Nevertheless, Edison's method was not silly, for at that time there was a limited knowledge of chemicals and their reactions. The long, hard way of testing may also have been the surest way.

Several busy months passed as Tom Edison and his assistants worked on, tested, and improved their various projects. By early fall, the group needed only to find the right metallic burner to replace the platinum. By then, Edison had tried over sixteen hundred different substances. It seemed he was indeed looking for a "needle in a haystack."

Finally, Edison went back to testing carbon—the same material he had started with a year before. Though he had tested carbon once after that, he had never tried it with the new Sprengel pump or the proper generator. Now, with the right energy current and fewer, if any, gases in the bulb, Edison thought there might be a different effect on the carbon.

One scientist who had tried using carbon in his own incandescent light experiments had made his carbon rod about one sixth of an inch in diameter. That scientist's experiments had not worked. Edison did his own calculations and figured that his carbon rod should be one sixty-fourth of an inch, or as thin as sewing thread. With a carbon rod that thin, Edison figured he could make the bulb glow with eight times less current.

For the next few weeks, Edison and his staff worked

at making the slivers of carbon rods. They purposely burned the inside of the gas lamp bulbs, for the burned black substance on the inside of the glass was carbon. They scraped off the carbon and mixed it with tar to hold it together. Then they set to kneading it with their fingers, as if it were dough. It was extremely difficult to make such fine threads of carbon, for it usually crumbled.

One day, an assistant became so frustrated trying to knead the carbon that he shouted out loud.

"How long did you knead it?" asked Edison.

"More than an hour," the assistant replied.

"Well, just keep on for a few hours more and it will come out all right," said Edison.

In time, Edison's staff could knead carbon rods even thinner than a thread.

At this stage, Edison and his staff experienced both great excitement and disappointment. They knew they were near the solution, and yet they had not reached it. Few assistants went home during that time, for work was never done. Instead, they took turns sleeping and working for a few hours at a time.

Edison's staff did not despair or complain about their long hours, for working for Tom Edison was an adventure to them. His positive attitude inspired them to keep trying. They also realized that their "captain" worked as hard or harder than any of them. He was always there during the toughest times.

By October, the men had made many experiments with the carbon rods. Charles Batchelor was best at putting the tiny carbon filaments into the bulb. It often took him hours to insert it, but his hand was always absolutely steady and his patience was strong.

In the meantime, Edison had turned to other sources for making the carbon rods. On October 21, he tried a cotton thread that he had burned in a special way. Once the thread was burned, Batchelor took the precious substance and carried it over to the bulb maker's bench. Just as he got there, the carbon broke. A few hours later, Batchelor had another carbon thread. This one was broken accidentally when a screwdriver fell on it. It was nighttime before Batchelor had completed inserting the carbonized cotton thread into the glass bulb.

Then, the current was turned on. The men waited to see how long the light would last. It seemed impossible for such a fragile filament to last long. They were expecting it to go off in the usual hour or two, but this time the light stayed on—and on. It lasted thirteen and a half hours!

The next day, Edison tried the same experiment with a different kind of thread—and the light lasted forty hours! The weary men jumped for joy. "We've got it! We've got it!" they cried.

Only Tom Edison was quiet. Then he said, "If it can burn that number of hours, I know I can make it burn a hundred."

On November 1, 1879, Edison applied for a patent (which he received two months later) for his incandescent, carbon filament lamp. The carbon that served him best came from a piece of hard, Bristol cardboard that had been burned to a hairlike substance. With it, his lamp had burned for one hundred and seventy hours!

It was not the first electric light, nor was it the first incandescent lamp. But it was the lamp Tom Edison had in mind all along—one that was practical and cheap to run and that provided the perfect bright light for a home.

Though no one outside Menlo Park knew it then, the age of electricity had begun.

CHAPTER FOURTEEN

Lights, Power, and Proof

Tom Edison wanted to keep his lightbulb a secret until he was satisfied that it was perfect. For many weeks, day and night, he kept working on his invention. But the more he kept quiet about it, the more rumors began to spread.

Edison's neighbors were the first to notice the new bright lights coming from his laboratory.

"They're much brighter than anything I've seen before!" they exclaimed.

"They burned all night, too!"

"No kidding! Really?"

"Edison's up to some new tricks, that's for sure."

Then train passengers, riding between New York and Philadelphia, also began to notice.

"Look, ma! That house has such bright lights!"

"Why, that's so! That's Thomas Edison's laboratory. I wonder what he's invented now."

As the word spread, and hope for another miraculous Edison invention grew, the price of Edison Electric stock rose to thirty-five hundred dollars a share. That price was many hundreds and thousands of dollars higher than the price of most other stocks.

Finally, on December 21, 1879, the story of Thomas Edison's light bulb was reported on the front page of the New York *Herald*. It called Edison's invention a "triumph" in lighting with electricity and declared that "a scrap of paper" made light "without gas or flame" and that it was "cheaper than oil."

If Edison had been well known before, he was now world famous. None of Tom Edison's earlier inventions, even the phonograph, amazed people more than the first light bulb.

But to Edison the light bulb was only his starting point. Now he could go on to develop his complete electric light and power system—one that would give homes heat as well as light. The public's reaction to the lightbulb helped Edison receive more money from his investors, which he needed. He wanted to develop an entire system over the next few years, and the bulb was just one part of it.

As Edison saw it, his power system would need many things. They included new dynamos, underground lines for distributing the power, safety fuses in case of short circuits, and insulating materials. Also, it would require new power switches, regulators for the generators, meters for measuring current, and many lighting fixtures and sockets. Finally, special wiring would have to be installed for homes. Before he could set up such a system anywhere else, he first needed to test it at Menlo Park.

As that project got under way, Edison also set out to find a better burning substance for his bulb. The Bristol cardboard he had tested was meant to be only temporary. Although the cardboard filament could eventually last three hundred hours, he knew that that was not long enough. In addition, many of the lamps broke down, and two inventors claimed that they had patented Bristol use in light bulbs before Edison.

Edison tackled this familiar problem with his usual energy and invention. Later, he said, "Before I got through, I tested no fewer than 6,000 vegetable growths and ransacked the world for the most suitable filament material." After several months, Edison found just the thing: bamboo. Bamboo proved to be both cheap and completely original. On top of that, it gave off a soft, reddish glow for up to *twelve hundred* hours.

Setting up the power system was difficult. There were many kinks to be worked out, equipment delays, and breakdowns. Also, Edison was forever changing plans or machinery in an attempt to make his system better and better as he went along. Nevertheless, Edison's longtime supporter, Mr. Lowery, urged him to have an electric light demonstration ready soon. People were tired of waiting to see what this "power system" was all about.

In December 1880, more than a year after he invented the light bulb, Tom Edison was ready to show his system to some New York City officials. His company, Edison Electric, had requested permission to establish its first power system franchise in New York and was seeking the approval of the officials. The demonstration would show the men the wonders of electric lights and electricity.

With Mr. Lowery's help, the demonstration went perfectly. Edison showed the men to the upper floor of his laboratory. The room was in complete darkness until Edison suddenly switched on the lights. New and fancy chandeliers immediately lit up, giving the room a lovely glow.

But something was wrong, Edison noted. The men did not seem at all interested or impressed. The trouble was, these city officials cared more about holding on to their jobs than about setting up Tom Edison's electric power system. They worried that Edison's system would force the gaslight companies out of business. The heads of these companies were rich and powerful men who had helped vote many of the officials into office. The gaslight men had warned the officials that allowing Edison's system in New York might cost the officials their support in the next election.

To make Edison think twice about setting up his power system in New York, the officials told him they would have to tax him one thousand dollars for every mile that his system extended. That made Edison angry. The gas companies did not have to pay *any* taxes!

No deal with New York City was made that night.

Basically, the gas companies feared the competition from Edison Electric. They made fun of electric power and tried to prevent its development. A better course, perhaps, might have been to buy the patents to Tom Edison's invention, just as Western Union had done years earlier with the stock ticker. That way, they could have avoided the competition by controlling the inventions themselves.

It is also likely that Edison would have sold his patents. At that time, he needed money to set up factories that would make equipment and accessories for his lamps. Without the factories, he could not possibly make enough lamps to sell to the public. Edison appealed to his investors for more money, but they stubbornly refused to support a new and untried business.

Seeing no other choice, Edison realized he would have to start up the factories himself. To raise money, he formed two different partnerships with his associates. He also sold some of his shares of Edison Electric Company, and sometimes he borrowed money from the company. Edison believed so strongly in what he was doing that he risked all the money he had in order to set up the electrical equipment industry. Many businesspeople doubted Tom Edison or thought he was plain crazy. Still, Edison knew his own mind.

By 1881, things were looking up. The Edison Electric Company had won permission from New York City to lay the underground power lines—without paying tax—throughout the city. It also got permission to distribute and sell electric light. To top that, the latest power system demonstrations at Menlo Park had so impressed the heads of the banking, railroad and telegraph industries that they gave Edison eighty thousand dollars. The money helped Tom Edison set up the first public power system. (In the end it cost six hundred thousand dollars.) The Edisons' new home would be New York City.

Not only would Edison be living in the city, but his headquarters would be on elegant Fifth Avenue. "We're up in the world now!" Edison exclaimed at that time. He marveled at how just ten years before he had arrived in that same city, penniless and without a place to sleep. "And now think of it!" he said. "I'm to occupy a whole house on Fifth Avenue!"

But Edison had little time for fun or even for being with his family. He was in New York to get people excited about electricity and his new system. He also wanted to perfect his system so that people would immediately want electricity rather than gas.

As expected, the gas companies put up a big fight. They tried to get Edison to leave. Edison ran into other problems, too. He needed to find the proper machinery and enough qualified people to help him with his work. Overall, though, Edison was thrilled at having this extraordinary opportunity to make his dream come true.

To begin, Edison covered a large wall of his headquarters at 65 Fifth Avenue with a map of New York City. For hours, he would sit and study a colored portion of the map. That section showed where he planned to install his first power station. The area included part of the financial district, for he hoped to gather the support of possible investors. It also included streets with small factories and housing for the poor. The first power station itself would be on Pearl Street.

In the weeks and months that followed, more information was added to the map. Edison had members of his staff go from door to door in the designated area to find out what the residents thought of electric power. People were asked whether they used gas in their house, and if they did, how much. Then they were asked whether they would change to electricity if it cost the same as gas.

His staff also reported the number of stores and factories that might want to install electric motors. All that information was put onto the map. In addition, the map showed exactly where the underground power lines were to go. Soon, the map showed Edison all he need to know: the amount of electricity that would be needed during the day and night.

The actual task of putting the power lines underground was extremely hard. It meant digging fourteen miles of trenches through the city streets. Edison was always on hand then. He made sure the lines were laid correctly and safely. Doing it the right way from the beginning, Edison felt, would prevent accidents later on.

Edison also had larger, more powerful dynamos built. The early ones at Menlo Park had been eight horsepower, which could light fifty lamps; the new jumbo dynamos were a whopping two hundred horsepower, able to light twelve hundred lamps.

The Pearl Street Power Station was ready to be opened in June 1882. Inside the station stood four enormous steam boilers, six steam engines of two hundred and forty horsepower and three (later six) jumbo dynamos. There were controls, switchboards and a thousand electric lamps with which to test the system. Crude meters were also installed to measure currents to individual customers.

"The Pearl Street station was the biggest and most responsible thing I had ever undertaken," Tom Edison recalled. "It was a gigantic problem," he said. Yet if it worked, the station would affect almost the whole world. Still, Edison was nervous about the public opening, because so many things could go wrong.

"All our apparatus, devices and parts were home-devised and homemade. Our men were completely new and without central-station experience. What might happen, on turning on a big current into the conductors under the streets of New York, no one could say," he said.

On top of that, he had to keep an eye on his enemies. "The gas companies were our bitter enemies in those days, keenly watching our every move and ready to pounce upon us at the slightest failure," Edison said.

In the end, the situation was this: "Success," Edison said, "meant worldwide adoption of our central-station plan. Failure meant loss of money and prestige and setting back of our enterprise."

For all those reasons, Edison postponed the opening day many times throughout the summer. He wanted to make sure everything was as perfect as possible. Finally, at 3 P.M. on Monday, September 4, 1882, Tom Edison gave the order to the chief electrician:

"Pull the switch!" he cried.

To an observer, it seemed the Edison lights around Pearl went on without the slightest effort. However, in the bright light of the warm, summer afternoon, the lights did not have much effect. Tom had purposely wanted to avoid a lot of publicity about the event, in case something went wrong. So the first lights on the streets of New York caused little public notice. The story was reported on the inside, not in the headlines, of the daily newspapers. Nevertheless, the reports were positive.

The article in *The New York Times* said, "It was not until about 7 o'clock, when it began to be dark, that the electric light really made itself known and showed how bright and steady it was." The *Times*, which had fifty-two Edison lamps in its offices, described the light as "soft, mellow, graceful to the eye; it seemed almost like writing by daylight."

Tom Edison's electric light and power business began slowly. At the time of his Pearl Street opening, he had only eighty-five customers, who had bought four hundred lamps. Though many people were amazed by the Edison lights and thought them better than a gas lamp, they considered them way too expensive at a dollar apiece. There were also certain kinks to be worked out, such as leaks from the circuit boxes on the street and other fire hazards.

In time, though, business grew along with recognition for Edison's achievement. It is important to remember, however, that Tom Edison alone did not invent the light bulb; he had the writings, knowledge, trials and failures of many scientists and inventors before him to use as a foundation for his own work. Tom Edison was, however, the first scientist to use that knowledge to make electricity, and to make electricity available to everyone.

On the day of the quiet but successful opening of the Pearl Street station, Edison exclaimed, "I have accomplished all that I promised!"

Perhaps it was an excess of pride in his achievement, however, that led to trouble for a few years later. An inventor named George Westinghouse studied the Edison electric light system and recognized some of its weaknesses. The Edison system depended on direct current, or DC, power. The main problem with DC power was that it could not generate much power over long distances; nor could it give off the industrial strength that more and more companies were demanding. Westinghouse saw the solution in alternating current, or AC, power.

The system of alternating currents basically took Edison's system one step further. Ironically, Edison refused to take that necessary step. Perhaps he did not understand the importance of AC currents because of their complex nature. Or perhaps Tom Edison did not want to recognize its importance, for fear that a new system would replace his own. For whatever reason, he seemed to have closed his mind to any further improvements.

Meanwhile, Westinghouse continued to study alternating current. He was aided by one of Edison's own former employees, a Serbian-American inventor named Nikola Tesla. Together, they and other associates struggled to win acceptance of this new system. Edison had fought the same fight years earlier in convincing people to choose electricity over gaslight.

For a while, Edison and his company were able to keep up the public's confidence in his direct current system. But in time, AC power was recognized as the better system, and the Edison company was forced to admit its mistake.

In 1896, Edison's company, then called Edison General Electric, licensed the alternating current patents from Westinghouse Electric. In return, Westinghouse could use any of the Edison electric patents.

This company truce ended what would go down in history as Tom Edison's greatest miscalculation.

CHAPTER FIFTEEN

Thomas Alva Edison—World Famous Inventor

At the age of twenty-four, Tom Edison had simply been one half of the stock ticker company Edison & Murray. By the time he was thirty-five, the name Edison was the only name attached to some of the most remarkable companies and products of the day: the Edison Electric Light Company, the Edison lamp, the Edison Machine Works and the Edison phonograph. The Edison Laboratory at Menlo Park was also well known as the "birthplace" of Tom Edison's most famous achievements.

The invention of the light bulb and the opening of the first central power station in New York marked a turning point in Edison's life. Though his name would go on to be associated with many more varied and important inventions, none could match his accomplishment in electricity.

Edison's family life soon changed as well. Throughout his years in Newark and Menlo Park, Edison had worked long hours. Sometimes he would not come home for days at a time. This made Edison different from most fathers with regular working hours.

Though Tom loved his wife, Mary, their marriage was not an easy one. Mary was a simple, gentle woman who had not had much education and could not understand the complex experiments on which her husband constantly worked. Tom wished he could share more of his life in the laboratory with her. Mary wished Tom would share more of his life with her at home.

However, the times they did spend together as a family were happy ones. Edison tried to be with his family on Sundays and often took them to a nearby beach, where they would picnic, play and enjoy the sun.

In the winter of 1883–1884, Tom Edison became ill and tired. Someone suggested that he go to Florida, where the climate was warm and soothing. Tom went with Mary and their daughter, Dot. They enjoyed themselves so much that the whole family went back the following winter.

But in the summer of 1884, Mary suddenly came down with typhoid fever. A few days later, she died.

After that, Edison never wanted to see Menlo Park again. His staff emptied the large, wooden buildings and closed the laboratory for good. Edison and his three children stayed in New York. This was a difficult time for Tom Edison. For the next two years, he lost himself in his work to forget his sadness.

During that time, Edison was introduced to many women. Because he was so wealthy and famous, Edison was considered a "prize catch." Women from all over the

United States came to meet him, hoping to become the next Mrs. Edison. Tom was polite to them, but for a long time, no woman interested him at all. He was not ready to marry again.

One day some friends introduced him to a young, 18-year-old girl named Mina Miller. Mina was the lovely, dark-haired, bright-eyed daughter of a successful inventor from Ohio. She had gone to a finishing school in Boston and had recently returned from a grand tour of Europe. Mina loved people and was interested in many things. After they met, Tom could not get her out of his mind.

During the next year, Edison was very busy traveling to different places. He courted Mina by sending her frequent letters. When he returned, he courted her in person. But being hard of hearing, Tom found it easier to talk with Mina in Morse code, which he taught her. They tapped out their conversations to each other by hand, and no one else knew what they were saying.

That system came in handy on a long trip to the New Hampshire mountains. They were traveling with three other people in the carriage, but no one heard Tom ask Mina to marry him. He had tapped the question out in her hand! She tapped back, simply, "YES."

Mina Miller Edison was well suited to be Tom's second wife, for she was accustomed to being around people and high society. Now that Tom Edison was a leader in American industry, he had new, public demands on his life. In the United States and Europe, many important people wanted to meet Edison. They held banquets in his honor and gave him medals and awards. Tom disliked those events, but Mina helped him through them.

Tom and Mina moved to New Jersey, this time to the rolling countryside of West Orange. There, they lived in a beautiful, red brick mansion on a large estate called Glenmont. Tom Edison felt this new home suited his wife, as well as his new position in life. Nearby, he built a new cluster of laboratories that was ten times bigger than Menlo Park. The books and materials there were so extensive that for a time the West Orange laboratory was the most complete private research laboratory in the world.

The new lab did not outshine the one in Menlo Park in the quality of work or inventions that came from it. Still, Edison continued to work on many large projects, often on several projects at once.

It was in West Orange that Edison renewed his interest in the phonograph. He had let that invention lie for ten years. By the time he picked it up again, people either had forgotten the machine or remembered it only as a curious toy.

Edison credited his deafness with helping him perfect the phonograph. He said, "The great defect of it was in copying overtones in music and hissing consonants in speech." Tom Edison knew that if his ears could hear the different overtones, and not the hissing sounds, the average person would enjoy the sound even better.

In improving the phonograph, Edison recalled, "I worked over one year, twenty hours a day, Sundays and all, to get the word 'specie,' perfectly recorded and re-

Mina Miller Edison, the house in Glenmont, and Thomas relaxing with a book.

produced on the phonograph. When this was done, I knew everything else could be done—which was a fact."

Meanwhile, Edison also began working on an instrument that, he said, "does for the eye what the phonograph does for the ear." This invention, which he called the kinetoscope, recorded and reproduced pictures of things in motion. This was the beginning of motion pictures, or movies, as we know them today.

Edison worked on his kinetoscope and improved it with a better film. Called Kodak, it had been invented by a man named George Eastman. Eventually, Tom Edison thought of combining the kinetoscope with the phonograph to make the first sound movies. And in 1897, Edison made the first color film by tinting each frame with a special paint.

Tom Edison worked on motion pictures until he had come up with the best movie camera possible. Though this machine was still large and bulky and was used only between 1890 and 1894, it became the model on which all modern movie cameras were based. Also, the size of the film Edison settled on—thirty-five millimeters in width—is still the standard size used in movies today.

Yet Edison was not the kind of person to stay with a project once he had perfected it. He preferred to turn his attention to new experiments and inventions. Thus, the motion picture industry grew from the work of other people, not Tom Edison.

The one disastrous failure in Tom Edison's inventive career was his iron-ore mining operation. From the early 1880s on, iron was in great demand; it was needed to make steel, which in turn would go toward making buildings, trains and other kinds of new industrial equipment. Edison himself had had to buy iron for his dynamos and had found it very expensive. He wanted to develop an iron-ore operation that would make it cheaper.

Edison bought land in the hills of the New Jersey and Pennsylvania border, where iron ore had been found. He centered his operation in the New Jersey town of Ogdensburg. For the next *ten years* Edison learned about mining and tackled its problems: engineering, rock quarrying and rock crushing. He also devised a moving conveyor belt, with rubber belting, which helped move the iron-ore rocks from one refining process to another. (Though there were conveyor belt systems in meat-packing houses in Chicago, it was only after reading about Edison's system that Henry Ford was inspired to try it out in his automobile factory.)

Despite all the time, sweat, effort and money that Edison spent on this operation, it did not succeed. Problems with the machinery and accidents caused by workers set back the work. And Edison found that in order to sell his iron at a cheap price, he had to mix it with other substances. Unfortunately, even after many thousands of experiments, this produced only a low-quality iron.

In the end, the 1899 discovery of an enormous supply of iron ore in northern Minnesota closed Edison's operation for good. The Minnesota supply was so great that the ore could be mined and sold cheaply in its natural form. But by then Edison had run through all his money—which had been in the millions of dollars. He was also in debt some several hundred thousand dollars more—all because of this mining project.

Naturally, Edison did not feel happy about what had happened. Still, he took his money loss in stride and said, "Well, it's all gone, but we had a heck of a good time spending it!"

By the time Edison came down from the rocky New Jersey hills, the automobile age had begun. Edison immediately saw the future in these "motored carriages" and knew that the horse and buggy would soon be extinct. At that time, gas-powered automobiles were the least reliable type of car, compared with ones using steam engines or electricity. Since the steam engine cars were heavy, and the electric ones clean, light and quiet, Edison predicted that all cars of the future would be driven by electricity.

Edison figured he knew enough about electricity to safely enter the automobile field. He studied the battery that then powered the electric car and saw that it had many faults. It was composed mainly of lead acid, which was heavy and not long-lasting. Tom Edison decided that he would make a battery like a "box of electricity." It would be light, long-lasting, able to recharge itself and economical.

Though Edison spent many years developing his battery specifically for the automobile, the final product was not at all well suited for it. By that time, electric cars had disappeared. Gas-powered ones had been improved and had taken their place. The Edison battery was not even

Edison gave his all to every project.

useful as a car starter, for it was not strong enough and it did not work well in cold weather.

The Edison battery did, however, prove extremely useful and rugged in many industrial areas. It was great as a backup source of power in power plants and for railway signaling. It provided energy for miners' lamps and train lights. Mining companies used it to blast away rock, and it was used on merchant ships and battleships during World War I. The Edison battery was also the first battery to power naval torpedoes.

Tom Edison gave his all to every project. Though inventors with a better business sense would have quit when they realized that profits would never match their investments. Edison did not have that ability. To him, the will to invent and create was far more powerful than the fear of losing time and money. His strong curiosity and keen observation always kept him supplied with new ideas.

Edison also had the ability to bounce back from defeats, like the ore-mining project, and to move ahead on new and better projects. He had so many ideas that he patented more than *one thousand* inventions or improvements on inventions during his lifetime.

Nor did disaster pull him down. At the age of 67, Edison watched his West Orange laboratories burn down in an accidental and horrendous chemical fire. But within three weeks the factories were largely rebuilt. Edison even hired employees to work in two shifts so that he could catch up on production of his most recent invention—a phonograph that played *disc* records. The order for these phonographs was worth almost ten million dollars. With his ever-positive and practical outlook, Edison did not waste time mourning the loss of much of his life's work. Instead, he salvaged what he could and rebuilt from there. He made the success outweigh the damage.

Nor did those qualities disappear with age. When Tom Edison was eighty years old, the automobile and rubber tire manufacturers, Henry Ford and Charles Goodyear, asked him to come up with a rubber substitute that would be cheaper and easier to obtain than real rubber. With the same dogged energy that guided him to invent the light bulb, Edison experimented with fourteen thousand plants that yielded some kind of rubber until he found the one he was seeking.

And whatever worked for Tom Edison soon added to the quality of life everywhere. His contributions can be measured in his drive, personal energy and courage to explore while others just stood by and shook their heads.

In the eighty-four years since the cold, snowy night of Tom Edison's birth, the whole pace of American life had changed. In that time, the United States had gone from horse-drawn covered wagons to gas-powered cars. Airplanes could fly overseas, and the first rocket had already been demonstrated. In 1847, the United States was still fighting the Indians over territory. By 1931, the United States had claimed victory in World War I and was on its way to becoming a world power.

Those years had been a time of enormous industrial expansion, and Tom Edison had been at the very heart of it. When he was born, pioneer towns and camps of covered wagons depended on oil lamps and candles. Now, some eighty years later, modern cities around the world were ablaze and alive with electric light. And from small towns to Times Square, there were movie theaters, record players, telephones. These were just some of the inventions that Edison helped to create or perfect, and each one added to the quality of life.

Thomas Edison was as much admired for his contributions to science and modern life as he was for his openness and desire to share his discoveries with the public. Unlike many men of science, Edison did not shut himself off from people. He let people see his laboratory and read about his efforts in newspaper articles. Edison's attitude helped create an awareness and an interest in science among people.

Edison was rewarded many, many times for his contributions. Even so, he did not care to be the center of honor and attention. Instead, he preferred to be at work, even when he was so old and sick that he was unable to get to the laboratory. After a banquet given in his honor in 1929, at which President Herbert Hoover spoke, Edison collapsed. As he lay in bed, he said, "I am tired of all the glory, I want to get back to work."

In his two remaining years, Edison stayed at home in New Jersey with his wife, Mina, and many servants. There, despite his ill health, he kept up with new technological advances, such as airplanes. He also studied and tried to understand such complex problems as the forces and uses of atomic energy.

It was Edison's own contributions that announced the great inventor's death on October 18, 1931. The telegraph, the telephone and the radio flashed the news worldwide, while newspaper reporters ran to their typewriters. Newsreels nationwide also carried the story.

There was one final, private tribute to the man who had brought electricity to homes and daily life. From the White House to the smallest cabin, people everywhere dimmed their lights at 10 P.M. on the day of Edison's funeral. For a moment the world was dark, as it had been for so many years before. Then, silently but steadily, the lights went back on, burning brightly against the night.

apparatus

A set of equipment used for a specific purpose. Electrical apparatus, for example, is a set of equipment used with electricity.

battery

A device that stores electric current. A wet-cell battery (a car battery, for example) contains liquid, usually an acid solution. A dry-cell battery (such as a typical flashlight battery) contains no liquid.

Bell, Alexander Graham

The man who invented the telephone and who started the Bell Telephone Company.

carbon

An important element occurring in many different forms. Diamonds, coal, petroleum and limestone are all mostly carbon. The black substance that collects on burned glass is also carbon, and this is what Edison scraped off and used in his telephone transmitter and in his light bulb filaments.

circuit

The complete path of electric current. It must be a closed loop, beginning and ending at the same place.

dynamo

A device that generates electricity; a generator.

eclipse of the sun

An event in which the moon passes directly between

the earth and the sun and casts a shadow on the earth. From the ground this looks like a black disk sliding over the face of the sun for a few minutes.

experiment

Process in which a scientist, following a careful plan and using controlled conditions, conducts an experiment to test a theory, make observations of how something works or make a discovery (for example, of an unknown element).

filament

The part of a light bulb that gives off light; a thread of carbon or metal that glows when an electric current passes through it.

gold indicator

A device similar to a telegraph used to quickly report changes in the price of gold to customers who make deals in the gold market.

horsepower

A unit used to measure the power of motors. Originally, one horsepower (often abbreviated as 1 hp) was the pulling power of one horse. A five-horsepower motor could pull as much as five horses.

incandescent

Glowing with intense heat.

incandescent lamp

An electric lamp in which a filament gives off light when heated by an electric current.

insulator

A material that is a poor conductor of electricity used to prevent current from flowing where it is not wanted.

Glass, wood and rubber are examples of good insulators.

invent

To produce something useful for the first time through the use of the imagination or through ingenious thinking and experiment.

investor

A person who gives money for the purpose of getting more money back in the future. For Edison, investors were the people who gave him money to support his work. When his inventions were successful, his investors shared in the profits from them.

laboratory

A place equipped to conduct experiments and scientific research.

Lincoln, Abraham

The sixteenth President of the United States. He was President during the Civil War.

Morse code

A code invented by Samuel Morse in which letters and numbers are represented by dots and dashes or long and short sounds. It was used primarily for sending messages by telegraph.

paddleboat

A boat used only on rivers, lakes and canals, which moves by means of a paddle wheel.

patent

An official government document that gives an inventor the exclusive right to make, use or sell his invention for a certain number of years. Every time an inventor invents something, he applies for a patent from the U.S. Government Patent Office right away. This means that if any person or company tries to copy and sell the invention, the inventor can take that person or company to court.

Pony Express

A rapid postal system that carried mail across the western United States in 1860 and 1861. It worked by using relays of horses and riders and was replaced by the transcontinental railroad.

scarlet fever

A serious contagious illness that causes inflammation of the nose, throat and mouth and a red rash.

static electricity

An electrical charge that builds up in one spot and does not flow until it is discharged all at once in a spark. An example of this occurs when a person shuffles his or her feet across a rug on a dry day. The action creates a charge of static electricity that is discharged when the person touches something and gets a shock.

telegraph

An electrical apparatus for communicating over great distances by wire, using coded signals (Morse code).

test tube

A plain tube made of thin glass closed at one end. It is used for experiments, especially in chemistry and biology.

Western Union

The large telegraph company that hired Thomas Edison first as a telegraph operator and later as an inventor. It still exists today.

Wizard of Menlo Park

The nickname given to Thomas Edison. Menlo Park was the town in New Jersey where Edison lived and worked while he was developing his electric lighting system.

1. One of Thomas Edison's great achievements was to design a system which brought electricity to private homes. Make a list of all the things in your home that run by electricity. Next to each one, write how the tasks it performs were done before electricity was available. Here is an example: light bulbs—candles, oil lamps.

2. Thomas Edison was a brilliant inventor. He imagined devices that could do things for people, and then figured out ways to build them. Imagine a new device that would do something for you. What would it do? How would you build it?

3. Thomas Edison was partly deaf. This was a handicap because it made it hard for him to understand people when they spoke to him. Yet this did not keep him from being a great inventor; in fact, it actually helped in some ways. Name some ways that Thomas Edison's hearing problem hurt him and some ways that it helped him.

4. Running a laboratory for inventing and improving new devices costs money. Edison had to pay his assistants, pay for the supplies he used, pay for the gas and water and pay for food for himself and his wife. How did Edison get the money to take care of all this?

5. When Thomas Edison was a boy, one of his teachers,

the Reverend Engle, said that his mind was "addled," or muddled and confused. Why did the Reverend Engle think this? Was he right? Why do you think that smart people sometimes don't seem as smart as they are to people around them?

6. Describe how Tom Edison's mother educated her son. Do you think she was a good teacher? Why?

7. It is important to understand that Thomas Edison did not just invent a light bulb, but rather that he designed an entire system of electric lighting for private homes and businesses. Describe how the first system he set up in New York City worked. From where did the electricity come? How was it delivered to homes and businesses? How did Thomas Edison know how much to charge each person who used his electricity?

8. Some people were not in favor of Edison's new electric light system. Who were they? Why were they opposed to it?

9. The light bulb was the most important part of the electrical lighting system Edison designed, and it took a long time to design and perfect. Review Chapters Twelve and Thirteen and answer the following questions. Notice how the invention did not come from a single flash of inspiration, but rather from a careful, scientific, step-by-step process.

—Why did Edison reject using arc lights for his electric lighting system?

—What was the problem with the first incandescent lamps?

—Why did the glass bulb have to be airtight?

159

—What was the problem with using platinum as a filament in the light bulb?

—What was the problem with using carbon as a filament?

10. Name three things besides the light bulb that Thomas Edison invented or improved. Pick one and describe either how it worked or how it worked better because of what Edison had done.

11. When Thomas Edison was a boy, the exciting new invention of the day was the telegraph. Describe what the telegraph did. Telegraphs were very important at the time, but they are not used much today. Why not? What has replaced them?

12. Do you think Thomas Edison could have invented as much as he did without the help of his assistants in the laboratory at Menlo Park? What did his assistants do? How did they help him? Give specific examples from your reading.

Blow, Michael. *Men of Science and Invention.* American Heritage, 1960.

Bolton, Sarah K. *Famous Men of Science.* Crowell, 1960.

Burlingame, Roger. *Inventors Behind the Inventor.* Harcourt, 1947.

Fanning, Leonard M. *Fathers of Industries.* Lippincott, 1962.

Halacy, P. S. *Science and Serendipity: Great Discoveries by Accident.* Macrae Smith Co., 1967.

Meyer, Jerome S. *Great Accidents in Science that Changed the World.* Arco, 1967.